Spirit Guides

Unlock the Secrets to Connecting with Your Guardian Angels, Archangels, Spirit Animals, Departed Loved Ones, and More

© Copyright 2021

The contents of this book may not be reproduced, duplicated or transmitted without direct written permission from the author.

Under no circumstances will any legal responsibility or blame be held against the publisher for any reparation, damages, or monetary loss due to the information herein, either directly or indirectly.

Legal Notice:

This book is copyright protected. This is only for personal use. You cannot amend, distribute, sell, use, quote or paraphrase any part or the content within this book without the consent of the author.

Disclaimer Notice:

Please note the information contained within this document is for educational and entertainment purposes only. Every attempt has been made to provide accurate, up to date and reliable complete information. No warranties of any kind are expressed or implied. Readers acknowledge that the author is not engaging in the rendering of legal, financial, medical or professional advice. The content of this book has been derived from various sources. Please consult a licensed professional before attempting any techniques outlined in this book.

By reading this document, the reader agrees that under no circumstances is the author responsible for any losses, direct or indirect, which are incurred as a result of the use of information contained within this document, including, but not limited to, —errors, omissions, or inaccuracies.

Your Free Gift (only available for a limited time)

Thanks for getting this book! If you want to learn more about various spirituality topics, then join Mari Silva's community and get a free guided meditation MP3 for awakening your third eye. This guided meditation mp3 is designed to open and strengthen ones third eye so you can experience a higher state of consciousness. Simply visit the link below the image to get started.

https://spiritualityspot.com/meditation

Contents

INTRODUCTION 1
CHAPTER 1: OVERVIEW OF SPIRIT GUIDES 2
    SPIRIT GUIDES TAKE MULTIPLE FORMS 3
    THE DIFFERENT TYPES OF SPIRIT GUIDES 3
    ANIMAL SPIRIT GUIDES 4
    GUARDIAN ANGELS 5
    ANCESTORS 6
    PLANTS 8
    GODS AND GODDESSES 10
    ASCENDED MASTERS 10
CHAPTER 2: GETTING TO KNOW YOUR ARCHANGELS 12
    THE SEVEN ARCHANGELS IN THE BOOK OF ENOCH 13
    OTHER ARCHANGELS YOU CAN CALL UPON 15
    HOW TO INVOKE THE ANGELS 18
CHAPTER 3: SPIRIT ANIMALS – HOW TO FIND YOURS AND
WHY IT WILL CHANGE YOUR LIFE 22
    WHAT ARE SPIRIT ANIMALS AND HOW DO THEY EXIST? 23
    FINDING YOUR SPIRIT ANIMAL 24
    ANIMALS CAN MANIFEST IN DIFFERENT FORMS 25
    THE QUALITIES SPIRIT ANIMALS BRING TO YOUR LIFE 26

CHAPTER 4: ASCENDED MASTERS AND SPIRITUAL TRANSFORMATION 32

WHAT ARE ASCENDED MASTERS? 32

WHO ARE THE ASCENDING MASTERS? 33

WHAT IS SPIRITUAL EVOLUTION, AND HOW DO YOU KNOW IF YOU ARE EXPERIENCING IT? 36

RECOGNIZE YOUR SPIRITUAL TRANSFORMATION 37

CHAPTER 5: HOW TO CONTACT YOUR DEAD LOVED ONES 42

CHAPTER 6: HOW TO FIND AND STRENGTHEN YOUR SPIRIT 50

HOW TO RAISE YOUR VIBRATIONS AND FIND YOUR SPIRITUALITY 51

CHAPTER 7: HOW TO CONNECT WITH YOUR SPIRIT GUIDES 58

STEP 1: IMAGINE WHAT YOU ARE ABOUT TO EXPERIENCE 59

STEP 2: SET OUT YOUR INTENTIONS 60

STEP 3: ASK FOR GUIDANCE FROM THE HIGHEST ORDER OF SPIRIT GUIDES 61

STEP 4: USE PRAYER AND MEDITATION TO LISTEN MORE INTENTLY 63

STEP 5: BELIEVE IN YOURSELF 64

STEP 6: WRITE THE SPIRITS 65

CHAPTER 8: WHAT HAPPENS WHEN THE HUMAN SOUL ENTERS THE SPIRITUAL WORLD? 67

STEP 1: THEIR ANCESTORS JOIN THEM 68

STEP 2: SPIRITS CAN LEAVE THE BODY WHEN THE TIME IS RIGHT 69

STEP 3: THE RESTING SPACE 69

STEP 4: THE LIFE REVIEW 69

STEP 5: TRANSCENDING INTO SPIRIT FORM 71

STEP 6: CONSIDER REINCARNATION 72

CHAPTER 9: SIGNS THAT THE SPIRITS ARE KNOCKING AND HOW TO HEAR THEM CLEARLY 77

SIGNS THAT THE SPIRITS ARE TRYING TO COMMUNICATE WITH YOU 78

CHAPTER 10: STAY SAFE WHILE COMMUNICATING 87

HOW TO REMOVE EVIL AND NEGATIVE ENERGY 88

SOURCES THAT ARE AFFECTING YOUR ENERGY 88

WHITE LIGHT PROTECTION 90

SMUDGING 91

WHAT ARE THE BENEFITS OF SMUDGING? 91

- How to Smudge 92
- Crystals and Gemstones for Protection 95
- The Best Crystals to Use for Protection and Their Properties 95
- Ideas for Your Spiritual Makeover 96

CHAPTER 11: SPIRITUAL PLACES AND TIMES 99
- Ways to Recapture the Joys of Your Childhood 100
- Spiritual Places to Visit 101
- Some of the Most Inspirational Places on Earth 102

CONCLUSION 108

HERE'S ANOTHER BOOK BY MARI SILVA THAT YOU MIGHT LIKE 109

YOUR FREE GIFT (ONLY AVAILABLE FOR A LIMITED TIME) 110

REFERENCES 111

Introduction

Do you consider yourself a spiritual person, or is it a world you have never visited? Current events and times of change have affected everyone, and some people believe that it is now time to expand their belief system. Spirituality is not just about connecting with another realm and detaching from reality; it's about utilizing all the available help. Imagine it as a host of spirits who are there to guide and protect you along the way! Spirits that are filled with love and wisdom are waiting for you to get in touch.

If you have ever experienced a feeling of déjà vu or that someone has walked over your grave, you may have already had contact with the spirit world. If you miss your relatives who have passed away or are simply curious about what lies on the other side, this book is ideal for you.

Even if you are already familiar with the spirit world and the guides that reside there, this book is filled with information to improve your experiences. Everyone learns lessons as they live their lives, which is also true of the spiritual realm. If you want to improve your contact with your spiritual guides and the rest of your divine protectors, jump in. The answers are waiting for you inside these pages!

Chapter 1: Overview of Spirit Guides

First, you must acknowledge that you need help. You may be one of the most capable beings on Earth, but you still need guidance and support from other sources. You may feel your friends and family give you the help you need, but what if you could call on otherworldly sources for help?

That is what spirit guides are. Some people believe they are assigned spiritual helpers and guides before birth, while others call on them when they need help. People who have formed spiritual connections will tell you that they are part of your subconscious and are the only way to find your wholeness. No matter your personal beliefs, you should keep an open mind when it comes to spirit guides.

Unfortunately, the elemental part of spirituality has been tarnished by commercial sources that dominate marketing and online content. The people behind the marketing have realized that while the world is hurting, they can make money from vulnerable people looking for help. If you feel ready to start your spiritual journey or are looking for a new experience to enhance your life, spirit guides will escort you.

Spirit Guides Take Multiple Forms

At their most basic level, they are archetypal energy sources. They exist all around you and in multiple dimensions. Some spirit guides will connect with you in a physical sense, while others rely on mental interrelation. You will experience different types of spirit guides at varying levels of intensity. Some guides stay with you for life, while others interact sporadically.

Multiple spirit guides will intensify your journey and help you find the path you need to take. They will warn you of dangers and teach you the wisdom to defeat your opponents. They are there to comfort you in times of sorrow and rejoice with you in times of triumph. They are not judgmental; they understand the human psyche better than you do. After all, they have been around since the dawn of time and have seen many generations of humans come and go.

The Different Types of Spirit Guides

Half Man — Half Beast

Also referred to as trans-species, many spirit guides will appear as this type of being. If you look at historical figures in religion, you can identify the more recognizable trans-species forms.

1) *Pan:* In Greek religion, Pan was the god of nature. He took the form of half-man and half-goat and was responsible for farmers, shepherds, and flocks of sheep. He was also responsible for the mountains, wildlife, and music and was renowned for summoning nymphs. With his sturdy hindquarters and phallic horns, he is regularly associated with fertility and sexual energy.

2) *Anubis:* Ancient Egyptians regarded Anubis as one of the most powerful gods of their time. He takes the form of a muscular black man with the head of a jackal. His ears are pointed, and his snout protrudes from his face. He is regarded

as the god of the underworld and the afterlife and is responsible for guiding lost souls and helpless beings. Anubis is not just part of the process of death; he is also a protector and guide. He promises that all souls who seek his help will be protected in the afterlife and offered sanctuary depending on how they have lived their lives.

3) *Ra*: Another god from Egyptian history, Ra is known as the sun god, representing growth and strength. He is depicted with a man's body and the head of a falcon crowned with a sun disc. The tree of life is reported to grow in Ra's temple, and humans were formed from his tears.

4) *Ganesh*: The Hindu god of success is depicted with a pot-bellied man's body with four arms topped by an elephant's head. As one of the most recognizable trans-species gods, he holds a goad in his right hand that helps him clear the path for his chosen followers. This means they will find the path to success and happiness. In his other hand, he holds a rosary that symbolizes the pursuit of knowledge. He is known as the embodiment of wisdom, education, and wealth.

Animal Spirit Guides

Later in the book, you will explore the role of animals in the spirit world. Their accessibility and your natural affiliation with the animal kingdom make them popular choices for spirit guides. Native Americans and the Chinese have a long history of animal connections and sacred representations. The totem poles in indigenous American culture would often be decorated with animals' images to represent the beliefs and lineages of individual tribes.

The Chinese used over thirty different animals to represent their beliefs. They would use the symbols to highlight a person's qualities and describe the negative aspects of their personality. Their totem animal was a dragon that was used to represent power. Most Chinese leaders wore robes adorned with the dragon image that gave the wearer a sense of dignity and power.

The Chinese zodiac is also associated with animal imagery. They have a twelve-year cycle that assigns a different animal for each period. Chinese people believe that your zodiac animal will have a major influence on your personality and success.

Guardian Angels

Also referred to as light beings, your guardian angel is assigned to you before birth—or so it is believed. Some people confuse religion and angels and believe that only Christians have access to angels. This is not true. Angels are non-denominational and available to all faiths. Atheists also have a guardian angel they can connect with should they feel the need. Angels respect freewill choices and are guided by them.

Every guardian angel is like a traditional nurturing mother. She will guard you with the strength of a lioness and watch over you from birth. It can be difficult to imagine what an angel is like. Popular media and the world of Hollywood have painted them as one-dimensional creatures that should be worshipped.

However, angels are highly emotional creatures who have a heart and soul. They are merciful creatures filled with compassion for humanity. They have an affinity for you because they chose you. They stood beside your unborn soul and pledged to guide you through life. They made this sacred bond fueled by love and an affinity with your soul. They may have lived former lives with your souls or have chosen this new incarnation for the first time.

It is important to understand that when you ask your guardian angel for help, you give them the freedom they need to help you unconditionally. Imagine them as spiritual butterflies that surround you, just waiting for a sign that you need them. They will never interfere with your free will or force you to do things you do not want to do. As a nurturing force in your life, they simply want the best for you.

Most people have more than one guardian angel that will come to their aid, depending on the nature of the problem. Think of them as the best bunch of friends you could have. There is the joker of the pack, who will have the positivity to pick you up when you are feeling down; their lighthearted, playful persona will help you regain your sense of humor. In contrast, there will be a wise, sensitive, and more serious one on hand to dispense pearls of wisdom to help you reach the right decisions. No matter how many guardian angels you have, they are all friends who know everything about you. Whenever you need them, they are there for you, as true friends who will guard your secrets with their lives and give you room to express your true feelings.

That is how you should view your guardian angels—as mother-like creatures that are also your best friends. Nonjudgmental and always forgiving, they will always tell you the truth and offer help. Further into the book, you will find out about Archangels and how to communicate with them, but guardian angels are already there. Acknowledge them and become accustomed to their presence, and you will know when it is time to connect with them.

Ancestors

Ancestral spirits are the spirits of dead relatives. As they leave their physical bodies, their souls rise and join the universal spirit realm. They are around to help you resolve any problems in your life and can be invoked using traditional rites. They will always be on hand to provide guidance and protection to their family members on the physical plane.

Ancestral spirits are traditionally a branch of the respect people have for their ancestors and form a direct link with higher beings. As they are already members of the spirit world who have resided on Earth, they can help you deal with more earthly problems like divorce, addiction, health worries, financial worries, and infertility.

Their goal is to help you achieve your full potential and become a successful human being.

Ancestral spirits will often visit you in the form of dreams. Various forms of ancestors will visit you and allow you to make connections with them. Ancestral spirits could be vague, shadowy beings that immediately make you feel at ease in their presence, or they could be the spirits of your grandparents. Have you ever been to a place and thought you recognized a member of your family for a second, only to remember that they've passed over, so it cannot possibly be them? Well, the truth is that an ancestral spirit might have visited you.

Meetings like these will leave you feeling safe and secure. Your memories of your ancestor should fill you with joy as you realize that you are part of a larger family experience. The messages they bring will be intensely personal and filled with references to your experiences with much-loved predecessors.

Ancestral spirits are more coherent than other spirit guides and have a real investment in your future. They will have an insight into your life that is deeply affected by family history. Ancestral spirits know your soul's history and are more concerned with your lineage than others. They want you to carry on the family name and help you choose the perfect partner to have children.

As they are relative newcomers to the spirit world, they won't be as spiritually advanced as other guides. They are more practical and mindful of modern ways, so ask them for help on raising your kids, coping with work, and paying the bills. They can also help heal any negative energy created by past misdemeanors in family history. When you are affected by negative energy at home, call on your ancestral spirits to heal the environment and make it homier.

Plants

Even though they are an intrinsic part of the living world, it can be a common mistake to dismiss the humble plant's spirituality. Native Americans understood the importance of plants and the spiritual meaning they represent. The sacred use of herbs and plants can be traced back generations.

In Europe, mistletoe was used to celebrate the Winter Solstice, and Wiccan believers carry on the same traditions today. Despite its toxicity, the plant was used to symbolize fertility and poison. The ancient Brits believed it represented immortality, while the Druids incorporated it into their rituals to ensure success.

Ancient Greeks and Egyptians revered the plant verbena. They believed it had magical powers and would allow them to connect directly with higher powers.

In the Americas, the use of peyote and mescaline in traditional rites certainly made things more interesting! These natural psychoactive plants were used to induce trances where the members of the tribes could speak with their gods and spirits. They also used white sage to induce hallucinations and connect with higher beings in a disassociated state.

In modern times, people now know the reasons behind these "spiritual" connections when using psychoactive plants and the science that explains such reactions, but they also know that the living world has formerly undiscovered connections. Plants can be used to enhance people's lives with their symbolic meaning, and they can be introduced into your diet for a more physical connection.

Some people form bonds with the spirits of plants in the same way they bond with spirit animals. If you have an affinity with certain plants or flowers, their spirit can affect you.

Different Ways to Contact the Plant Spirits

1)   *The Call of the Green:* Shamans believe that plants are constantly trying to speak with us. Try taking a trip into their world to hear them. Take a walk in the wild, somewhere like a forest or open field, and listen with open ears. If you state your intention to find a spiritual bond with the plant world, they will respond.

When you reach out for help from the plants, they will share with you their specific healing qualities. They can treat your mind, body, and spirit by combining your psyche with their spiritual senses.

1)   *Gazing:* Once you have formed a bond with plants, you will want to intensify the experience. This can be achieved by the shamanic practice known as "gazing." Simply merge your consciousness with that of the plant and feel their mindfulness. Become a part of the plant and feel the strength of its roots and how they secure it to the earth. Feel the effect the wind and sun have on the plant and the constant sense of growth it feels. As you become part of their being, they become part of yours. Feel the sap and natural warmth they share with you and let it fill your soul.

2)   *Treat Them with Respect:* Modern research conveys that plants have feelings and will respond to actions. This means that you can have intelligent, valid interactions with all the plants in your life. Treat them with love, and they will respond by flourishing and bearing fruit. They have invited humans to become part of their incredible world to share their healing qualities with them. Surely that invitation should be accepted with joy!

Gods and Goddesses

Study any given culture, religion, or belief system, and you will find higher beings that are classed as gods and goddesses. They can take many forms and are worshipped, feared, and obeyed in every part of the world. Norse religion differs as it considers the gods and goddesses as part of their extended family and would never consider prostrating themselves in front of them. Instead, they embrace the flaws and the powers the gods' show and recognize the traits that made them more human.

Christians believe that God has seven different spirits: the original spirit, wisdom, understanding, advice, knowledge, strength, and fear. These interpretations are from the Book of Revelation in the Bible. Christians believe that the number "7" has spiritual connotations, and it appears regularly in religious texts.

You will learn about the more approachable spirits of gods and goddesses in a later chapter.

Ascended Masters

These spirits have lived on Earth and have undergone a spiritual awakening that has transported them to a higher plane. They are believed to have transcended the process of reincarnation that the rest of humanity undergoes. Instead, they have taken their rightful place in the spiritual world and are now available as spirit guides to humans.

While they represent the ultimate teachers and the wisest of all spirits, they will still answer all mortal calls. They do not limit their wisdom and knowledge to those deemed worthier. You can call on such luminaries as Jesus, Confucius, Krishna, and other ascended masters whenever you need their help.

The spirits of ascended masters are also referred to as cosmic masters and ascension teachers credited with achieving the ultimate state of consciousness known as Divine Consciousness. They have mastered time and space but continue to learn from mortals. Just because they have reached such high levels of spirituality doesn't mean they have become separated from people. In fact, they recognize the need to intertwine with them and help them achieve the next step on their path to spiritual awareness.

There are thousands of ascended masters you can call on, and this subject will be expanded on later. You can choose your preferred member of the ascended host, depending on your requirements. The ascended masters are there for the benefit of humankind and will always answer your call.

Chapter 2: Getting to Know Your Archangels

Angels have been part of the human belief system since ancient times. They have been depicted on Egyptian tombs, Greek artifacts, and items scattered around Asia Minor. People experiencing near-death situations have been known to report them.

Those who have encountered angels fall into two camps. Some people view the existence of angels as a theological fact. They refer to the Bible and other religious texts to support their beliefs and provide religious evidence of angels and how they give guidance to humankind. Some accept the existence of angels as a philosophical dogma. They don't need to back up their beliefs with evidence because they believe angels can exist; therefore, they are extant.

In the Abrahamic faiths, the term archangel means "chief angel," and only two were named directly in the Bible. Gabriel and Michael appear within the canonical book, yet there was mention of the seven archangels in the Book of Enoch. This chapter will discuss the seven prime archangels and then beyond. There aren't a specific number of archangels, but it is believed that there are at least seventeen that can be summoned to aid with guidance.

The Seven Archangels in the Book of Enoch

Michael

Known as the angel of protection, Michael is the supreme leader of the angelic hosts and the only angel to appear in the Torah, the Qur'an, and the Bible. He's pictured as a warrior angel armed with a sword of righteousness and a shield of light. He's also often referred to as God's champion and the slayer of dragons.

He will protect you from chaos and evil in both physical and psychic form. He is a physical powerhouse who is the first-line defense for God against Satan and all his demons. He doesn't claim to be wise or knowledgeable and relies on his strength to protect his charges.

If you need protection or are feeling vulnerable, you should reach out to Michael.

Gabriel

Referred to as the strong one, Gabriel is the ultimate messenger between the divine and earthly regions. It is unknown whether Gabriel is male or female, so the angel is often depicted as an asexual being. Angels are energy sources, and followers may require a male essence one day, and a female essence the other. Gabriel's most important role within the Bible was when he appeared to Mary to inform her of the birth of Jesus and the role he would play in God's plan.

If you wish to connect directly with the angels, Gabriel should be your starting point.

Ariel

Known as the Lion of God, Ariel rules the animal kingdom and plants of the world. She is personally responsible for the four elements and strives to create harmony among all living things.

If you feel deeply about the ecological problems the world is facing, you should contact Ariel and ask for her help to protect Mother Nature.

Azrael

Recognized in several forms, Azrael is known as the angel of death or destruction. His role is to comfort those souls who are stuck between the worlds of life and death. He is often referred to as the keeper of the void and provides help to cross this important boundary. Some people believe that Azrael is causally linked to the Grim Reaper, but others dispute this fact. Azrael doesn't decide who will die; his role is to offer relief to those who have passed and the people they leave behind.

Azrael is the bookkeeper of births or deaths and is responsible for keeping a report on earthly life and all aspects of humankind. If you are missing a loved one who has passed, you should ask for his help to cope with your grief.

Raphael

The angel responsible for healing and wellbeing, Raphael oversees the medical community. He is one of the few angels who have attained saintly status within the church. He is the patron saint of the sick and provides compassion and care alongside healing powers.

If you are suffering from an illness or disease that is causing you pain and mental anxiety, you should call on Raphael to come to your aid. He is also known as the protector of travelers, so if you are embarking on any kind of journey, physical or spiritual, you should ask for his help.

Jophiel

Also known as Sophiel and Iofiel in certain beliefs, this angel is responsible for beauty and wisdom. She can be dismissed as a trivial angel concerned more with physical beauty than other spiritual matters, but she's a positive force and will help you leave behind negativity through the power of natural beauty.

If you ever feel lost in admiration at the wonders of nature, this could be the work of Jophiel. She will help you heal negative situations and restore inner calm.

If you want to clear your headspace and fill it with positive energy, invoke her power, and embrace her creative energy.

Chamuel

While Gabriel is the ultimate messenger between the realms, he is the angel who recognizes more practical connections. He's the search function of the angelic world that will hunt for whatever it is you need. He has been described as the eyes of God as he's responsible for knowing where everything is at any given time.

If you are feeling lost or at odds with the world, pray to Chamuel. He will help you bring peace to your life in whatever way you need it. This could be related to personal relationships, peace of mind, or worldwide events. If you are searching for inspiration or a physical object, he will come to your aid.

Other Archangels You Can Call Upon

Metatron

Considered the angel of life, he is responsible for protecting the tree of life and recording humans' good deeds. He also records the events that happen in the heavens and notes them in the Book of Life.

If you feel you are in a rut or have a big decision to make, you should consult Metatron. He's also responsible for helping adolescents to make the transition into adulthood.

Haniel

The joy of God, Haniel, is one of the most helpful angels available. She is the protector of souls and will help you discover your purpose in life. She has an affinity with females and is dedicated to helping women cope with their menstruation cycles.

If you want to become more intuitive and a successful clairvoyant, Haniel can help you achieve that.

Muriel

Her name means the "perfume of God," and she is responsible for emotions. She will answer any call for help and is renowned for her compassion. She will form a strong connection with you and be there when you need her.

If you are suffering from emotional distress and need help with your mental health, Muriel will give you the support you need.

Uriel

Often described as the fire of God, Uriel is also known as the angel of wisdom. He stands close to God and will help you develop a strong connection with the Creator. He stands at the gates of the Garden of Eden and watches over his territory with wind and thunder. This archangel is a strong conductor that will help you connect with the spirit world.

If you feel your personal vibrations are poor and you want to form better connections, call on Uriel for help.

Zadkiel

The angel of forgiveness is one of the most important angels in Heaven. He will help you bring joy and freedom into your daily life and increase your personal vibrations. He will also help you forget the past, forgive your enemies, and move forward with your life.

If you are stuck in the past and filled with negative energy, consult Zadkiel. He will bring his energy and fill you with positivity while cleansing your spirit.

Jeremiel

He was one of the original seven angels chosen to interact with humans but has become one of the lesser-known archangels. This is because he is better at communicating with the mind rather than through speech. He is the master of mental imagery and visions and complements the archangel Michael by using symbols and dreams to accentuate the more physical means of communicating.

His name is directly connected to the mercy of God, and he can connect you with the wisdom of Heaven.

If you are suffering from negative emotions or harmful memories, you should ask for the guidance of Jeremiel. He will give you mental clarity and help you reflect on life lessons.

Sandalphon

This archangel is one of the most approachable angels in Heaven. He is the guardian of nature and will often manifest in this manner. He uses music and prayer to communicate with humans and will become your personal connection with the spiritual realm. He is a wonderful ally to creative souls and helps them with their projects. Writers, musicians, and painters will benefit from his help as he can raise the vibrations that form the energy behind their work and turn it into a divine presence.

If you need to connect with a down-to-earth angel who will immediately make you feel comfortable, Sandalphon is your angel of choice. His guidance style is gentle yet firm, and he will help you feel grounded while still maintaining a spiritual connection with divine beings.

Sachiel

Known as the angel of wealth and success, Sachiel has been kept under the radar but is now stepping up to take his rightful place and support humanity. His energy is a bright light that also soothes the human soul. He brings hope and purpose to the lives of those who have lost faith and lack direction. He believes that abundance should be available to everyone, but not just financially.

His guidance will help humans become a stronger life force through their connection with the planet. He has a powerful relationship with both animate and non-animate objects and will help you form bonds with animals, plants, oceans, and your community.

It is believed that he has entered people's awareness in recent times to help them confront the damage they have caused on Earth and repair it. He is the angel that will teach you how to ascend the monetary values that rule your thoughts and begin to change how you live. He will help you change the world slowly and bring harmony and assistance when needed.

If you want to improve your spiritual growth and leave materialistic desires behind, you can ask for Sachiel's guidance.

Orion

Named after the third brightest star in the universe, Orion is one of Heaven's lesser-known angels. He has always been serving Earth but has recently stepped forward to offer his energy more readily. Once you engage him, you will find yourself a chatty companion who is easy to hear.

Orion can clear your negative energy and fill you with a sense of inner truth. He will often appear as a glowing light, just like his name suggests. He'll also help you become an awakened cosmic being and share his wisdom with you. He can give practical and helpful advice to release your negativity and embrace positivity.

If you are finding it difficult to achieve your dreams and want a helping hand, contact Orion. He is more than willing to be your companion for every step of the journey.

How to Invoke the Angels

If you feel the need to invoke angels, the process is quite simple. You can use meditation, candles, and incense to enhance the experience, but they are more for your benefit than the angels'.

The main thing to remember is that the angels are waiting for you and all you must do is ask them in, but you do need to raise your vibrations to form a more successful connection.

There are many ways to raise your vibrations that include diet, exercise, and meditation, and these should all be considered part of your daily routine. When you are invoking angels, your surroundings can also play a major part in raising your vibrations. Remember that increasing your vibration is an ongoing process, and there is always room for improvement.

Be kind to yourself and open your heart to love and compassion. Learn to let go of the past and refocus your energies on positive outcomes.

Setting the Scene for Invocation

1) Choose a safe space. You need to know that you aren't going to be disturbed so that you can relax fully. Remember, the angels are waiting for you, and you want to be fully engaged when they answer. If you can perform the invocation in natural surroundings, you will be one step closer to the angels.

2) Close your eyes and fill your heart with light. Imagine it surrounds you and lights your physical form. Now imagine the light flooding into your veins and organs, so you become a flowing entity connected with your environment.

3) Picture your heart and the energy that surrounds it. Feel your heart expand and vibrate with love. Now picture the chakra that emanates from your heart and let it expand and connect with your spirituality.

4) Recognize your awareness. Now is the time to become wholly immersed in your experience. Let go of any thoughts or emotions that aren't relevant to your connection with the angels. You need to be fully cognizant of what you hope to achieve, and all other distractions should be left behind.

5) Imagine your inner light traveling to the heavens and connecting with the divine beings that are waiting for you.

6) Breathe, allow your mind to relax, and feel your inner vibration connecting with the light and path it has formed.

7) Now, it is time to call the angels and ask for their help. Try this simple invocation:

"I call upon the angels, archangels, and guardians who inhabit Heaven to connect with me now. I call upon them to help me elevate my vibration and strengthen my connection with the divine world. I open my heart and soul to the powers and wisdom they offer me, and I welcome the guidance and support they offer. Thank you to the divine being for allowing me to enter this spiritual world and make connections with His favored angels."

You should now be aware of your psychic connection with the heavenly world. This is the time to increase your focus and control your breathing. You are now ready to make your experience a personal connection with your angel of choice. Different angels choose varied ways to connect with the human world. Jeremiel, for instance, will form a mental bond and may connect with an image or a daydream that conveys his message.

Some angels rely on clairaudience and will connect with voices, sounds, and aural messages from beyond. This can be in the form of music, or maybe the sound of a bird singing. Nature has some amazing sounds to share, and the angels love to use them to communicate.

If you are known for the ability to follow your instincts and believe in your gut feelings, the angels may choose to connect in a clairsentient way. They will send you energetic transmissions that affect the information you need. You will instinctively feel the advice and help the angels are bestowing upon you.

Once you have formed the connections you require, the angels will always be there for you. Prayer and mantras will help you reconnect with them when the time is right. Contemplation combined with prayer will help you form a strong spiritual bond with your archangels and make them your constant companions through life.

Every practitioner will find their own way of connecting, and their preferred methods will differ from others. Some people use crystals, runes, and sigils to help them visualize their spiritual connection. All rituals are personal journeys into the spiritual world and should be designed to form the most effective route to the heavens.

Angels are benevolent beings and won't punish you if you get it wrong. They understand human nature and are eager to help mere mortals become more spiritual. They want you to access spiritual planes and explore your higher self. Some people simply must sit still, breathe deeply, and then ask to be connected with the angels, and it will happen. Other people will have to work a bit harder and use props and tools to form their connections.

There are no hard-and-fast rules for invoking angels. Use your intuition and emotions to determine the best way to summon the angels. Sincerity and emotional investment are more powerful than any magical tool or ritual. The angels know if you are going through the motions or not wholly invested, and they will not respond to your requests.

Remember, the angels are waiting to help, and if your request is from the heart and filled with good intentions, they will validate it and answer your pleas.

Chapter 3: Spirit Animals – How to Find Yours and Why It Will Change Your Life

Once you are ready to meet your spirit animal and welcome the energy it brings into your life, you will know. Your life will have reached a point when you recognize that material help and support has got you to that particular point, but there is so much more out there.

Finding your spirit animal is a heady experience and an utterly amazing spiritual awakening. You will be transported beyond the Earth's physical planes and introduced to the worlds that lie in the spiritual realms. You will know in your soul when you are ready to transmute into this realm and improve your relationship with the spirit animals that inhabit it.

How Will Spirit Animals Change Your Life?

- *Courage*: You will be imbued with a heightened sense of courage that will help you move forward with your life. You will be able to let go of toxic relationships and form bonds with people who make you happy. If you feel you are stuck in a rut at work, this courage will help you find a new job that is more satisfying and pays better.

• *Communication:* Spirit animals know how to communicate with all people. They can make the shyest and most timid soul bloom. They will pass this ability on to you and make you a better communicator.

• *Strength:* If you are making bad choices in life yet lack the strength to change, your spirit animal will help you find an inner power to overcome your demons. If addiction and depression plague your life, they will help you find your joy.

• *Wisdom:* Everyone makes mistakes, but the trick is to learn from them. Spirit animals have their own form of wisdom that they will share with you.

What are Spirit Animals and How Do They Exist?

First, it is important to study the human form before discovering how to connect with spirit animals. Science may seem like a strange place to start a spiritual quest, but it gives you the basic connection that forms spiritual relationships. All humans have DNA matches with animals and plants. Everyone is intertwined and form the family group that is classed as living things.

This means that it is a natural progression of thought to how everything is connected by cells. It's just a short step to realizing that, as humans, people send an S.O.S. to all other living things so that they feel their distress. This is how individuals ask for help from spirit animals to make them feel more connected.

Think of your connection to your spirit animal as a family thing. Take your immediate family and the things you have in common. How are you like your parents? Do you have brown eyes like your mom or hate pickles just like your dad? Now, look at the bigger picture. You are literally related to every other living thing on the planet.

Put simply, within your human makeup, you have memories of what it was like to soar the skies like an eagle. You have a cellular memory of what it is like to be a cat, an owl, or a spider.

When you feel the need to find these connections, you are seeking to restore the parts of your being that have become fractured, injured, or lost. Finding your spirit animal will help you rekindle the power you have inherited from your animal ancestors and use it as your power.

Finding Your Spirit Animal

Meditation

Connecting with your animal spirit can occur during meditation. Follow these simple steps to invoke your spirit animal to connect with you.

1) Choose a spot that is comfortable and free from interruptions.

2) Invite the four directions to join you. Use a phrase like "Welcome North, East, South, and West. I invite you to aid me in my quest. Mother Earth and Father Sky, you are also welcome to accompany me on my journey."

3) Lie straight on the floor to allow the passage of energy to flow through your body as you listen to a soothing soundtrack, like running water or nature sounds.

4) As you relax and feel connected with the earth, ask your spirit animal to appear to you.

5) As they make contact, thank them for their time and welcome them to your world.

6) Ask them if they are your spirit animal and guide and if they have any messages for you. If they reply affirmatively, let them know you are ready for all messages, even if they are difficult to know.

7) Once they have connected with you and delivered their messages, thank them for their connection and ask if you can do anything for them.

8) Once the session with your spirit animal has reached a natural conclusion, you will slowly return to the physical world. Take time to readjust to your surroundings before thanking the four directions and the earth and sky for their help.

9) Take a ten-minute break to collect the thoughts and messages you have been given.

10) Journal your experience and include all the details you can remember. This is especially important in early meetings as you can then revisit the experience and learn more from the meeting.

Animals Can Manifest in Different Forms

Your spirit animal may choose to place physical clues that will help you identify your connection. If you find that images of horses appear in films, books, or conversations, this could mean your spirit animal is trying to form a link. Similarly, people report red admiral butterflies appearing to them in unseasonal weather or unusual places.

Dreams

Spirit animals love to talk with people when they are asleep. When you are in a resting peaceful sleeping form, you are more open to trust your intuition and be less skeptical than when you're awake. The spirit world recognizes that sometimes humans need to take baby steps when accepting the presence of spirits. That is why they choose to interrelate during your slumber.

The Qualities Spirit Animals Bring to Your Life

Below are some of the more common spirit animals and what they can do for your spiritual health.

1) *Bear*: The immense strength of the bear can help you find your inner toughness. They relate practically to the Earth and being a healing force for the party. They will help you find the grounding force that you can call on when you are feeling unsure. Bears are a symbol of action and leadership that will provide you with an iron will.

2) *Butterfly*: These beautiful creatures embody personal changes. Think of how they emerge from their pupae form and transform into colorful beings that can soar into the sky. If your spirit animal is a member of the Lepidoptera family, you have struck gold! They will help you implement changes in your life to allow you to transform and appear to soar above your problems.

They also signify the need for fun and playfulness in your life. If you are too caught up in serious stuff, a butterfly spirit animal will help you rediscover the joy of living.

3) *Cat*: Everyone knows cats are independent yet can be loving and faithful. This is true of cat spirit animals that will bring curiosity, adventure, and independence into your psyche. They will also teach you the virtue of being patient.

4) *Coyote*: This animal spirit is filled with contradiction. It can be viewed as the joker of the pack and will bring lighthearted energy and a sense of humor to your spirit. It represents the balance between humor and wisdom with a hint of playfulness. When a coyote appears in a physical form, they will project their foolish side to put your mind at ease.

5) *Crow*: This magnificent black creature is associated with mystery and enchantment. If you invite this bird to be your spirit animal, it will guide you toward a higher plane. Crows are also intuitive and will support you with your dreams and expectations.

6) *Deer*: These gentle, graceful animals will seek to connect with humans who are sensitive and intuitive. They bring power and strength to your spirit and allow you to become more vigilant and avoid danger. These swift-moving animals can cover large distances with grace and seemingly effortless motion. They will impart these qualities to your inner spirit and aid you toward success.

7) *Dolphin*: Perhaps one of the most iconic spirit animals, they represent harmony and peace. Their keen intelligence means they prefer to connect with humans who are imbued with an inner strength yet have a calm and restful countenance. The dolphin spirit animal will protect those they are in tune with and help them find their natural peace and harmony.

8) *Dragonfly*: These colorful creatures are renowned for their strong wings and multi-faceted eyes. This makes them adaptable and joyful at the same time. Those who connect with the dragonfly will experience a strong connection with nature, which will help them shine. Their true colors will emerge, and they bring the ability to transform their character.

9) *Fox*: Some people associate the fox with a cunning nature, but the spirit animal is quite different. They use their natural intuition to help humans deal with tricky situations. Their perception is naturally heightened, and they bring a sense of awareness and guilt.

10) *Frog*: This spirit animal is associated with change. They remind people that transitions are essential to moving forward, and it is normal to grow as humans. They have ancient wisdom that they will share with their connections and are also blessed with strong emotional ties. They bring a feminine element to

people's energies and help them cleanse their auras and spiritual energies.

11) *Hawk*: These spiritual animals will often connect with people who are required to have strong observation skills and be adept at seeing situations from various angles. Firefighters and other members of the emergency services will benefit from hawk-like wisdom and a sense of perspective. They help people to clear their vision and improve the power of focus.

12) *Horse*: This is the most motivational of all the spirit animals. They bring a spirit of sexual energy, passion, and a taste for freedom. There are two forms of spirit animal represented by the horse, depending on what the human needs. They can appear as a wild being or a more restrained force. Horses will bring a sense of privilege and entitlement to those who need a boost to their self-confidence.

13) *Hummingbirds*: These tiny creatures should not be overlooked due to their size. Even though they are the smallest form of birds, they have a huge spirit presence. They have immense strength in their wings and are willing to share that strength with humans they connect with. They are independent, joyful, and filled with a sense of fun. If you connect to a hummingbird, you will immediately feel uplifted.

14) *Lion*: When you need a fighter in your corner, you turn to the spirit animal in lion form. While nature teaches that lions can be lazy, the spirit animal is quite different. They will bring you the courage to face adversities and advise when aggression is required. If this animal appears to you without being summoned, it can mean that your life is about to spiral. They are offering you support when times get crazy.

15) *Owl*: In nature, owls are often referred to as the upright, wise, all-seeing creature with binocular vision. Their spiritual forms bring similar gifts. They allow you to see past traditional barriers and get a clearer picture. They are intuitive and wise and

have an innate knowledge of deception. You can call on an owl spirit to help you.

16) *Panda:* While this bear's soft fuzzy appearance invites feelings of familiarity, the truth is much more intense. Their tranquil stance and slow-moving strength fill their relationships with humans with a sense of gentle strength. They bring good luck and peaceful vibes to everyone who reaches out to them.

17) *Panther:* If you are lucky enough to have a panther as your spirit animal, you will be protected by the fiercest of guardians. They bring a celestial force with their connections to the dark moon and the night sky. Their liaisons are filled with powerful symbolism, and they can represent death and rebirth.

18) *Sheep:* These gentle spirit animals will seek kinship with humans who have lost contact with their inner child. They feel their innocence and lack of guile leave them open to societal pressure. The sheep's presence indicates their need to return to simpler times and become a childlike version of themselves.

19) *Snake:* Many cultures respect the snake and the connection it has with life forces. They recognize that a snake spirit guide can help you connect with your primal self and become energized by its force. Snake spirit animals will help you discover the right path to take when you need to transition to another plane. The guidance will also include opportunities to heal along the journey.

20) *Spider:* With their amazing powers of weaving a strong web from the flimsiest materials, they embody the female energy. This doesn't mean they are exclusively available to women, as they are a source of strength for both sexes. They will connect with people who have the same creative skills and high receptivity. Spiders will teach you how to lay a simple trap to catch your prey. This skill can be particularly useful when seeking a mate or defeating an enemy!

21) *Tiger*: With its rolling gait and powerful haunches, the tiger is a magnificent beast governed by natural aggression. The spirit animal will also have a sense of personal power and help you connect with your inner feelings. It will teach you to trust your instincts and act on them swiftly. Tigers know that predictability can lead to disaster in the natural world, so they will help you adapt to the environment you find yourself in.

22) *Turkey*: These strange-looking birds represent the symbol of abundance. Often found representing times of plenty like Thanksgiving and Christmas feasts, their spiritual presence will bring you nourishment. This can be physical if you are recovering from an illness or, in a mental sense, grieving. They bring you the recognition that you should nurture not just yourself but your community.

23) *Turtle*: While they seem cumbersome on land, turtles are adept at traveling in water. This energy type will appeal to people who feel trapped in their earthly roles and seek the freedom associated with nature. Turtle spiritual animals will bring emotional balance and the courage to move forward. They are also humble creatures that will only emerge when they feel they are needed. If you feel like the world is overwhelming you and need to find a different life pace, you could appeal to the turtle for help.

24) *Whale*: In the spirit world, the whale spirit animal is the bookkeeper of the earth. It is tasked with recording all that happens on Earth and every interaction between living and spiritual beings. This is no simple task, so if a spiritual whale animal appears to you, it is time to take a closer look at your own life. The whale is organized, can communicate with all levels of beings, and is a natural historian. Use the skills they offer to become less dismissive of the truth that surrounds you. Their presence could be an indication that you need to open your eyes and be more aware.

25) *Wolf:* Whenever spirit animals are discussed, one of the most iconic images will be the mighty Canis lupus with its magnificent coat and glowing eyes. The wolf is a feral being with an inbuilt appetite for freedom. They can work in packs, but they are most effective when they are the lone operator. Wolves will often appear to remind you to trust your instincts and rely on your intuition. They are aware of the power of social interaction, but they will also remind you that isolation is not necessarily a bad thing.

These are the most represented animals in the spirit world, but that does not mean this is an exhaustive list. Don't be surprised if your incantation or evocation brings forth contact with an animal that doesn't appear on this list. The animal kingdom is filled with masterful creatures that know how to respond to your soul's cry for help, and it has a whole menagerie of animals to choose from.

Your particular spirit animal could be as diverse as an anteater that helps you with problems or a crocodile that shows you how to adjust your emotional energies to enhance your life. A humble grasshopper could signal your need for luck, while a peacock could bring a sense of self-worth and confidence in your life.

You get the picture; the animal's physical aspects are often linked with the spiritual elements they bring.

Chapter 4: Ascended Masters and Spiritual Transformation

What are Ascended Masters?

They are spirits who lived as humans and attained a spiritual transformation that has propelled them beyond the karmic cycle. They have paid off their karmic debt and mastered their association with their higher selves. Ascended masters have been through their allotted reincarnations and emerged from them with the wisdom and power to become a revered spiritual master and guide.

As they traversed through the spiritual plains, they have mastered the limitations placed on physical bodies and gained a wealth of wisdom through their various reincarnations. Everyone is looking to improve their spirituality and experience the initiations of ascension, and ascended masters are there to help you.

While improving your spiritual growth and taking a journey of self-discovery can be enlightening, it can also be an isolating experience. If you are struggling to find the support you need from your friends and family, it may be time to call upon ascended masters to help you embrace the challenge that lies ahead.

Who are the Ascending Masters?

Jesus Christ

Perhaps the best-known ascending master of all, Jesus spent time in the wilderness battling his demons and contemplating his spirituality. He was sent to Earth to walk among humans and teach them his blessings. He was sacrificed to save humankind and ascended to the heavens after his death.

He can instruct you in the arts of unconditional love, healing energies, forgiveness, and constancy. He will respond to prayers and visit you in your dreams or when you are meditating. Jesus is truly the ultimate ascended master.

Milarepa

This famous Tibetan yogi's full name is Jetsun Milarepa. His story is famous in Tibetan folklore and has been retold through generations of followers. His early history was a violent one, and he turned to murder to satisfy his need for revenge. As he became sorrowful about his past deeds, he sought to redeem himself through religion.

The yogi turned to recognize his sincerity yet also knew that he must atone for his past. He sent him trials that were both soul-destroying and designed to test his character. Milarepa completed his tasks with honor, and a tower he built is still standing in Tibet. He underwent a series of abusive onslaughts alongside his trials and emerged with a lack of negative karma.

He then spent time in solitary contemplation in the caves of Tibet and visited mountain retreats to gain an insight into his concept of reality. He later said that his time alone helped him find the path of true faith and spiritual enlightenment. Milarepa is the perfect example of how a life can change from a sacrilegious one to a sacred life in just one lifetime. He is credited with living the most rapid path to the Tantric life.

Saint Francis of Assisi

Born in 1182, Francis was baptized as a child of God, which angered his father, who preferred the world of business to religion. He drifted through his early life as a well-liked individual who didn't do well in school. He lived a sinful life filled with wine, women, and song.

His turning point happened during the period of history known as the Fourth Crusade. He was twenty-five years old and dressed in a glorious suit of armor, ready to go to battle with the enemies of France when God visited him. He had a dream that told him he was following the wrong path, and he should return to his village and rethink his life.

Less than one day had passed since Francis had left covered with glory and assured of a knight's triumphant return. His father and family were furious with his actions, which they perceived as shameful and cowardly. This didn't deter Francis, and he retreated to a life of solitude in a cave where he wept for his sins. God visited him regularly and filled him with grace until it was time to leave the cave and embark on his new mission.

He spent years following God's commands and embracing the less fortunate along the path of life. Eventually, he began to preach, and although he was never a priest, people flocked to hear him speak. He lived a simple life begging for food and living in the open air, and he encouraged others to follow his lifestyle. He also encouraged rich people to share their wealth with the poor and live by the Gospel.

Francis believed in preaching by his actions. He didn't want to abolish poverty; he wanted to make it holy. One story tells of him encouraging a man who had been robbed of his food to pursue the robber and offer him his robe.

His love of nature and animals was apparent to all, yet others chose to exploit his love. When he returned to Italy to spend his final years in his home country, he founded a brotherhood in his name, which had a membership of over 5,000 in his absence. He found the pressure from followers to conform to less rigid standards difficult to live with, and he handed over the authority of the brotherhood to others.

Francis's final years were filled with suffering and illness as years of poverty and simple living took their toll. He began to lose his sight, and his hands and feet were covered with stigmata to signify Christ's marks during the crucifixion. He died in 1226 at the age of 45 and was canonized as the saint of ecologists and animals.

Lady Portia

Also known as the ascended master, Lady Portia is the feminine aspect of the flame of transformation. She is responsible for inner peace and stability and can be called upon to restore harmony. She helps people raise their vibrations from the lower levels of criticism, judgment, and negativity to higher vibrations, including love, compassion, and justice.

Lady Portia will also help you with issues concerning:

- Understanding karma and banishing negativity
- Finding a personal balance between work and leisure
- Finding forgiveness when dealing with others
- Self-forgiveness and self-love
- Learning how to fulfill your dreams and discover your self-purpose
- Regain power over your actions
- Help with any legal troubles

Lady Portia is especially powerful in helping women achieve their aims and is an inspirational power in spiritual realms. She has a dedicated retreat known as the Cave of Light that nestles in the Himalayas, which she shares with Manu, who also has a cave in Transylvania named the Rakoczy Mansion.

A book named *Magic Presence* describes a group of followers' journey and their visit to the caves. It describes American believers entering the cave and being charged with natural life forces and elements that uplift their souls. They witness miracles and demonstrations of alchemy over 48 hours before emerging, having undergone a complete spiritual rebirth.

What is Spiritual Evolution, and How Do You Know if You Are Experiencing It?

Think of yourself as a vehicle. Your body and mind are the physical aspects of the vehicle, while your spirit is the driver. Just as driving a car is a learning exercise, and you get better as you gain experience, so is the spiritual journey through life. When you drive a car, it is important to avoid obstacles in your path. Driving through life is no different, and as you ascend through spiritual levels, you will notice differences in how you view certain events.

The journey through life has a final destination—inner peace. As you master techniques and improve your communication skills, you will become a master driver. You will instinctively know the path to take and the ones to avoid. Instead, you will choose a peaceful route that is pleasant to travel. Call it the expressway to Heaven.

The ascending masters above have a common bond that appears in their history. They all took time away from their lives to contemplate and regroup, mostly involving caves. Even though caves are not readily available for modern society, you can still take time to retreat. Finding a sacred space to discover your inner peace will help you travel a smoother path to your inner peace.

Recognize Your Spiritual Transformation

1) You Become More Aware of How You React to Negative Aspects of Your Life

Some people believe that the desire for happiness is one of the major roadblocks that stop them from making rapid spiritual progress. It is important to understand that suffering and trauma will help you evolve, and the pain you feel will help motivate you to a higher level of spirituality. Most people experience negativity daily and believe it is a normal occurrence. You need to learn how to embrace your suffering and turn it into a positive force.

2) You Lose Interest in the Shallow Aspects of Your Environment

If you find yourself reading a book or watching an informative program on television rather than partying with your friends, you could just be getting old! Or you could be evolving into a spiritually mature being.

Do you find yourself becoming bored with gossip and celebrity culture? Society is obsessed with celebrities and filled with images of how they live and love, which dominates the news. Maybe you enjoyed this at one time but are now finding yourself sickened by the shallow conversations that surround you.

Unfortunately, you will experience a period of feeling lost and lonely as you transcend the ordinary pursuits of those less spiritual than yourself. This will pass, and the discovery of your spiritual fulfillment is more satisfying than any worldly reward.

3) You Embrace Solitude and Spend Long Periods Alone Without Feeling Lonely

If your idea of heaven is a vacation in the woods surrounded by nature, this could mean you are becoming more spiritual. If you once thought the ideal vacation involved a crowded beach filled with partygoers followed by noisy nightclubs with drinking into the early hours but now shun these types of events, you are evolving.

Silence and solitude help you block out the distraction of a noisy world. If you prefer to choose a place of beauty and drink in the wonders of a natural phenomenon, you are quickening your spiritual transformation.

4) You Become Less Inclined to Follow Trends

If you feel frustrated by people's sheep-like mentality and prefer to buck trends, you are growing. You need to take a leap of faith and leave your comfort zone. If you are filled with a sense of wonderment about what lies ahead, you are filled with the strength of the spirits.

5) You Are Open to All Religious Concepts and Seek to Develop a Deep Understanding of Worldly Beliefs

If you have experienced a need to question what you believe and compare it to other cultures, this is a sign of spiritual growth. As you learn more, you realize the holes in your knowledge are huge. As you learn more, you also realize that reading is not the way to spiritual revelations. You begin to crave the experiences that will link you with the spirit world and are more willing to invoke higher beings with different cultural rites.

Don't worry if you feel your original beliefs begin to crumble. That is a good thing. They will form the foundation for higher truths as you begin to build your new belief system.

6) You Find Violence and Negativity Unacceptable

Modern media is filled with violent imagery and tales of murder and death. If you find yourself becoming repulsed by these images and horror, you are experiencing a spiritual awakening. Why are people entertained by images of horror and negativity when the world is filled with beauty?

This sudden change may come as a shock to you initially, but it will help you realize beauty and serenity in the media. You just have to find it. You will be drawn to movies and television shows that are positive and filled with joy, and you may turn to classical music to enjoy the simplicity of the compositions. You will know what path to take and when to take it.

7) You Begin to Experience Your Emotions Deeply

This can be a cause of concern to many people seeking spiritual growth. They question why they feel so depressed and experience inner turmoil on their quest. Some people believe that the road to self-enlightenment is filled with light and happiness and they become confused by their deep-rooted feelings of sorrow.

The truth is that long periods of depression often signal a significant breakthrough in the process.

They signify that you are becoming more aware of the negativity surrounding you and the need to rid yourself of it. It signifies the purity of your intentions and the need to cleanse yourself of negative forces. The feelings of euphoria that will follow such a cleansing will make the periods of sadness worth the effort.

8) Your Goals Change

When you undertake this spiritual journey, it will become clear to you that materialistic things bring extraordinarily little joy. If you begin to question who you are rather than what you want to be, your perception of fulfillment is changing. When you begin to seek improvements to yourself rather than your surroundings, you are on the right path.

9) You Are Physically Exhausted and Need More Sleep

Releasing negativity can take its toll on both your physical and mental energy levels. This can lead to the release of hormones within your system that overstimulates your senses. While this can feel euphoric at the time, it can also be exhausting. Accept that you need more rest and make sure you get the sleep you need. If you fight the natural desire to sleep, you may lack the energy to release the suppressed emotions. This could mean you run the risk of reigning in your emotions and having to start the process again.

10) You See the Beauty Around You

This is a telling sign that you are making great progress on the path to inner peace. If you find yourself shedding tears over the simplest objects, you have opened your soul to simpler perceptions. If you can see the beauty in a concrete post towering over an urban landscape, you are well on your way to spiritual advancement.

11) You Want to Make a Difference

The spiritual awakening is all about becoming a well-balanced person who understands the joy and suffering of the world and wants to make a difference. These feelings can manifest in many ways. Feeling the need to volunteer for local charities, donate money or time to needy causes or simply share your thoughts with others are all signs of compassion.

When you turn selfishness into selflessness, you are far along the path of your spiritual journey.

12) You Start to Contemplate Life After Death

Death is inevitable, so why do humans fear it? Talking about death and what happens to souls once they depart this mortal coil can be taboo in some circles. When you talk with spiritually mature people, they will happily talk about the afterlife and what they expect to find there.

Once you have strengthened your spiritual muscles, you realize that no matter what happens to your mortal body, a part of you will live on forever. This revelation will help you travel forward and continue to improve your quest for inner strength.

These types of questions should be asked when you are at your most comfortable. Try meditation techniques or a solitary retreat to give you the chance to ask the most important call of all: What will happen to you when your physical self dies?

If any of the above situations are relevant to you, you are already on a spiritual awakening path. These things take time. Allow yourself to accept these changes and remind yourself that for every feeling of sorrow and solitude, you will be rewarded with multiple feelings of joy and love. Seeking inner peace is a journey that is not taken lightly. Ask yourself why you are doing it, and the answers should help you overcome any obstacles you come across.

If you need further help, appeal to the ascending masters. They have all encountered times of doubt and been subjected to hindrances along their path to spiritual awakening. They are ready and waiting to help you reach your goals.

Chapter 5: How to Contact Your Dead Loved Ones

The spiritual world is a fascinating place filled with spirits ready to communicate and help you on your earthly journey. But what if you want to speak to someone in particular? Maybe you have lost someone recently and find yourself with unanswered questions you would love to ask him or her. Maybe someone passed over before you could visit them for a final time, and you want to say goodbye.

Spirits from the other side could also want to form a personal connection with you and tell you how your relatives are coping with the spiritual world. Whatever the reason, there is a way to resolve your issues by contacting your loved ones from beyond the grave.

Some people find the process of speaking to the dead terrifying, while others recognize how comforting it can be. If the thought of ghosts and spirits from beyond frightens you, ask yourself why. These relatives didn't terrify you before they died, so why should you fear them in spirit form.

Talking to the dead and contacting spirits has too often been portrayed in film or television as a scary process riddled with dangers. While it is true that bad spirits exist and can be summoned, if you keep yourself safe, you have nothing to worry about. All the safety aspects will be covered in a later chapter, so, for now, you will concentrate on different ways to contact loved ones who have died and passed over to the spiritual realm.

Crystal Ball

Often used in clairvoyance and scrying, the crystal ball is a safe way to talk with spirits. You can visit a medium and ask them to talk with your relatives, or you can try to contact them yourself. Crystal balls are available online from reputable sellers of metaphysical items, or you can get them at Bed, Bath, and Beyond! The choice is yours. A good crystal ball should be made from glass, amethyst, or smoky quartz. It is merely a tool to be used to make contact with the other side and help you focus your inner eye.

How to Use a Crystal Ball

- Cleanse your chosen space with essence and dim the lights. You may want to light candles and play spiritual music to help you focus your mind.

- Place the ball onto a stand or dark cushion.

- Gaze at it intensely and try not to blink. If you love to see images in Magic Eye pictures, you will know what to expect next!

- As time passes, you will begin to see images within the mist that forms.

- As the mist clears, the images will get clearer.

Now you need to analyze the images you saw. Do they have specific relevance to any family members that have passed, or do they mean nothing to you? Remember, you have not specified whom you want to contact for the first session, so don't expect to succeed on your first try. You may see images, words, or just colors, and only time will tell. Ask yourself how these images make you feel. What emotions do they conjure up? Fear, love, hope, and despair are all common feelings.

Once the reading has finished, you need to charge your ball. Leave it on a windowsill at night in full moonlight. Never leave it exposed to sunlight and optimally charge it for three nights.

Wrap your ball in a soft cloth and store it in a dark place away from prying eyes. Never let anyone else touch your ball, or you will get contrasting energy levels. This can lead to inaccurate readings and negative images.

Use Candlelight to Speak to the Dead

Take a large white candle and place it in a holder. Now place two pieces of paper close to the candle that say **YES** and **NO**. Now light the candle and sprinkle salt on the melted wax as you focus on the person you want to talk with. This binds the spirit to the candle and allows it to be used as a conduit.

Now ask if the spirit is with you. If you have made contact, the flame will flicker and lean to the paper with **YES** written on it. Now you can use the candle to ask questions. The spirits will use the rippling of the flame to indicate different emotions, and it is up to you to interpret their answers.

Summon the Dead with a Spell

This method is not for the fainthearted and involves some serious involvement. If you want to make sure the spirits will come through and stay with you for three days, you need to follow this powerful spell.

Take five green candles and light them. Now take a red rose and pluck five separate petals from the flower. Make a small bonfire and cast the petals on it. As they burn, take a small knife, and prick your left thumb, so that drops of blood form on the skin. Drip the blood onto the candles without extinguishing the flames and use the following chant:

"Spirits of the other world, I call to thee for help. I wish to use your all-seeing power to visit with the spirit of (insert the name of the person you want to speak to) and consult with them for three moons. Free them from the dark and let them see the light."

Finally, extinguish the candles' flames with the juice of lemon while thanking the spirits for their aid.

Use a Chant to Summon a Lost Sister

Female spirits are naturally drawn to female gods and their energy. If you have lost a female member of your family, like a sister or mother, use the power of the female gods to help you reconnect. You may have already formed a bond with some better-known goddesses, so you should appeal to them to find the spirit of your lost sister.

If this is your first attempt to talk to the female gods, choose a benevolent one like Freya, Iris, or Minerva. Try a chant like the following:

"Goddess (insert name of a goddess), I appeal to your feminine strength and benevolence to help me with my search. I yearn to speak with my absent sister (insert name of female spirit) and reconnect our feminine energies. She is my blood, and we share the power of sisterhood. Return her to me, and I will fill my heart with love and power for you."

Summon Family Witches

If your family has a history of magic and belief in the spiritual world, they will respond to a call from you in the physical world.

Draw a pentagram on the floor with chalk and place white candles at each point. Draw a circle of salt around the area to keep the energy positive. Ask other members of your family to join you in the area and hold hands. Chant together the following incantation:

"Family members, we appeal to you from our earthly plane to join us from beyond. Matriarchs, patriarchs, and their kin, we ask you to bless us with your presence to share your otherworldly knowledge with us. We seek to draw strength from our familial ties and make our lineage strong."

This spell/chant will soon uncover if anyone from your ancestral past had magical powers and a psychic streak.

Use a Sacred Space to Talk to the Dead

If you live a busy life and have a family, you will know how difficult it can be to find a peaceful place to connect with the spirits. If possible, you should create an oasis of calm in your home that you can retreat to whenever you feel the need. This can be as small or large as practicality dictates.

The garden can be a great place to create your nirvana, considering it is already a natural space. Clear a small area and create an altar from natural materials like stone or wood. Place your favorite crystal or a candle on the altar, ready for use. Now face north and thank the gods of the North for their presence. Repeat the sequence for the remaining three points of the compass.

Place a rug on the grass and use it to meditate until you feel ready to ask for help. Now state your intentions to the spirits and wait for them to reply. The incantation can work better if you are holding a picture of the person you are trying to connect with or an item that meant something to them when they were alive.

If your sacred space is indoors, try to create natural light inside. Open windows and use a sage stick or incense burner to dispel negative energy. Decorate the space with familiar objects and pictures. Use music and spiritual noises to help you focus your energy as you ask the spirits to find your lost relative.

Use Tarot Cards to Communicate with Your Relatives

Those who are familiar with tarot readings understand the importance of guidance from past relatives. They are the spirits that know you best, so they will give you the most accurate answers.

If you are new to tarot, there is a simple exercise you can try to see if your energy is attuned to your ancestors.

Remove all the Major Arcana cards from a deck of tarot cards. These are known as the trump cards and are numbered zero to twenty-one, which leaves you with twenty-two cards to deal with. Discard the other 56 cards and shuffle the trump cards. While you shuffle, ask your relatives for help and advice. Now ask your question and pull a card.

The cards you deal will indicate the following answers:

- *The Fool*: If you are considering a risky move, just do it! Don't worry about what others think; you will be okay!

- *The Magician*: Your thoughts are all over the place; sort it out!

- *The High Priestess*: You need to work on your mental development; physically, you are fine.

- *The Empress*: You need to step up and give your friends and family the help and support they need.

- *The Emperor*: Your time to lead has arrived. Grab every opportunity to shine and show your true worth.

- *The Hierophant*: Take note of advice from your elders. They are wiser than you, and you should listen carefully to what they have to say.

- *The Lovers*: Your life should be filled with activities and people who love you, and you love back. Discard anything that doesn't fill you with joy.

- *The Chariot:* Time is of the essence; get a move on, or you could miss your opportunity to put your plans in motion.

- *Strength:* Caring for someone is not a weakness but make sure they aren't deceiving you. Don't take any BS from anyone.

- *The Hermit:* You may be frightened to leave your current relationship, but you should know that it's better to be happy and alone than to let others make you miserable.

- *The Wheel of Fortune:* Good luck is on the way, so don't lose hope.

- *Justice:* Karma is a great leveler. People always get what they deserve in the end.

- *The Hanged Man:* Sacrifices will be rewarded. If you need to give up your time, cash, or energy to move on to other things, you will profit from the next stage of your life.

- *Death:* Always stay true to your character. If you change to suit other people, you will become a lesser person. These decisions may cost you friendships along the way, but the cost will be worth it.

- *Temperance:* You need a haven to retreat to when the world gets ugly.

- *The Devil:* Human nature is the strongest force in your body. Just because other people tell you your desires are non-conformal, you shouldn't listen. Follow your heart and grab every opportunity to fulfill your desires.

- *The Tower:* Don't mourn the destruction of your ideas. Rejoice in the opportunity for growth it gives you.

- *The Star:* There is always room for hope. Even the most desperate situations have a positive spin.

- *The Moon:* You should be able to make informed decisions based on scant details. If you spend too much time seeking answers, you may lose the opportunity to have a choice.
- *The Sun:* Success is in your future.
- *Judgment:* Quick decisions are not always bad ones. Even the most important decisions should involve swift conclusions.
- *The World:* The year ahead will be epic. Things are going to change for you beyond your imagination.

The key to all these methods is to persevere even when you feel you have failed to make a successful connection. Practice makes perfect, and as you try different methods, you will know which ones you feel more comfortable with. If the tarot cards do not make sense, it means that your relative's input isn't as strong as you need it to be. Try dealing the cards again and asking different questions.

Finally, even if you don't get immediate images or answers, be prepared to have some interesting dreams in the days following your attempt. Spirits often find it easier to communicate during the hours you are asleep.

Chapter 6: How to Find and Strengthen Your Spirit

Have you ever met someone who bowls you over from the second you meet them? Is a force of nature that fills you with joy, makes you grateful to be in their company, and does not need to be loud or in your face? Do they simply radiate goodness and love? If so, you know they are good people who aren't afraid of anything and are capable of whatever they put their minds to.

These people have a higher vibration than others. They are spiritually in tune with their inner selves, filled with positivity and love, and vibrate on a higher plane, which attracts people to them like moths to a flame. In the spiritual world, higher vibration is also the way you attract spirits.

A higher vibration tells the spirits you are ready to receive them, and you welcome their wisdom. You are in the right frame of mind and ready to step on the path to spiritual awakening. Fear is the main cause of a low and short vibration, so it is important to dispel the things that make you fearful. You need to fill your life with joy and make your vibration sing!

Raising your vibration is not difficult, but it can take time. If you have lived your life ruled by fear, it will turn negativity into positivity. You will need to remind yourself constantly to stay on the path of positivity and be prepared to forgive yourself if you step off for a while. Everyone is human with human emotions, and the best thing you can be is kind to yourself.

How to Raise Your Vibrations and Find Your Spirituality

1) **Count Your Blessings**: Are you constantly worrying about what you don't have? Are you focused on what other people have rather than what you are grateful for? Change that mindset and create a list of things you should be grateful for. You can create a section in your spiritual journal or dedicate a whole book to the subject.

2) **Write Something Positive:**

- *Your Family*: How do you feel when you think about your family? Are they the perfect support group, or are they a bunch of individuals with such different personalities they all have different qualities?

- *Your Friends*: Do you have a bestie? Why do you love them so much? Which of your friends is always there for you when you are down?

- *Your Courage*: You have lived your life with courage and have overcome many heartbreaks and pain.

- *Your Strength*: Life isn't easy. You have survived it so far, so your strength is apparent. Use your strength to grow as a person and become stronger.

- *Your Mind:* You are blessed with a complex mind that can transport you to places you have never been and help you solve the most difficult problems. Your mind is a major part of who you are, so be grateful for it.

- *Your Tears:* Do you remember the last time you cried? Was it because you were sad, or were they tears of joy? Your tears are badges of honor to mark the best and worst times of your life. Contrary to some people's beliefs, tears do not signify weakness; they show emotional strength.

- *Your Mistakes:* Yes, you can be grateful for your successes, but what about your mistakes? Own them and understand what you learned from them. This attitude will make you more determined to try new things and welcome change.

3) **Create**: Sometimes, life and work can be overwhelming. You work, you go home, and you look after your family and yourself. You then relax and sleep before another day on the treadmill of life. So, when do you find time to be creative, to let your talents flow, find new outlets, and learn new things? Find time to do something fun like cooking new recipes, creating art pieces, or learning a new musical instrument. When you find things to stimulate your inner sense, your mood elevates. This raises your vibration and makes your outlook more optimistic.

4) **Give Without Receiving:** When you give something from the goodness of your heart, you don't just feel a warm glow; you also raise your spiritual vibration. You can financially donate to a charity, or you can give your time by volunteering. Maybe you know someone who has been having a rough time lately, and you can help them. Just giving without expecting a reward will help you feel more spiritual.

5) **Use Your Words Wisely:** Your words are possibly the most powerful weapon you have. When you speak ill of anyone or even yourself, you are setting yourself back on a negative energy

path. Gossiping, complaining, and being unkind to others doesn't achieve anything, but it will lower your vibration. Use your words to raise your spirit and be kind to people. Compliments and encouragements are much better for your inner psyche.

6) **Exercise and Movement:** When your body feels sluggish, so does your soul. You need to incorporate plenty of movement into your daily routine. Take a brisk walk among nature to raise your vibes. Appreciate the beauty of your surroundings as you get your heartbeat rising. Feel the crispness of the air and the warmth of the sun. Nature and exercise should fill your soul with love and positivity and get that vibration rising!

7) **Just Let It Go:** If you consider yourself a victim whom others have maligned, that is how you will be treated. Nobody else has control of your life. They may have the power to influence certain aspects of your life, but ultimately you are in control. When you hand this power to others, you are always fearful about what they will do. Take back the control and learn how to let go of this fear. Forgive people for what they have done to you in the past and acknowledge the power shift.

8) **Create a Rule for Life**: Everyone needs a spiritual roadmap with a specific destination. This is your rule of life and a guide to connecting with your higher self, your true power, and your spirit guides. This isn't meant to be a strict plan, but it should be a fluid and changeable guide to inspire you when you feel a bit lost. Use a journal to note down prayers and mantras you can use to lift your spirits. You can also include meditation techniques you find especially helpful.

9) **Change Your Diet:** The foods you eat affect how you look and act. A healthy diet is important to keep your body active and fit for a purpose. Fresh, healthy ingredients mean you digest more nutrients and vitamins, so you function better. Can food affect spirituality, though? The simple answer is, "Yes, it can." As your vibration moves up a level, it can adversely affect your body.

As frequencies are raised, you can feel unstable and shaky. Your dreams may become more vivid and disturbing while your emotions are heightened.

The foods listed below will help you nourish your body to support you through this process. The pineal gland in the human body is often referred to as the third eye, and it needs certain nutrients to help it function correctly.

- *Healthy Fats*: When you add natural healthy fats to your foods, you establish contact with nature that helps ground you. Coconut, almond, and olive oils will all make your food taste amazing and support your nervous system.

- *Cacao*: This is a true superfood! It is from the purest part of the cocoa bean and can be taken as a supplement or used to create amazing food you will love. It contains a potent detoxifying agent that will help you clear your body and soul. It removes negative energy and dispels toxic energy. Cacao provides you with high energy levels without suffering the aftermath of a crash. Replace sugar with cacao wherever you can and benefit from its nutritional properties.

- *Beets*: These amazing vegetables will help you clean your system and repair any damage to the pituitary gland. They are packed with nutrients and contain antioxidants as well as anti-inflammatory properties. You can eat them raw or cooked, and they make a colorful addition to your dishes. The juice of beetroots can be a healthy alternative to fruit juice in your diet.

- *Herbs*: These easy to grow plants aren't just a quick way to make food taste better; they are key ingredients in your diet that will help you with ascension symptoms. You can add them to food or use the dried leaves to make herbal teas. Try rosemary, nettle, thyme, basil, and chamomile to help soothe you and move your vibration through higher levels of consciousness.

- *Water*: Staying hydrated is essential. Ascending can be tough on your body and cause uncomfortable side effects. When you drink water, you help your brain function, which supports your pituitary gland's health.

What you add to your diet is just as important as the things you leave out. Avoid fluoride, sugar, alcohol, processed foods, fast foods, fried food, and any products that have been treated with pesticides. Your body is your temple, and you must fill it with worshippers who will help you ascend rather than drag you down.

10) **Spend Time with Loved Ones**: The way you spend your leisure time is vital for your spiritual enhancement. Sometimes, people take their loved ones for granted as they are constantly seeking new connections and experiences. While it is important to put yourself out there and meet new people, you must look after the people who love you. Spend quality time with them over a shared meal or just relax together and talk.

It may sound clichéd, but you can forget to keep romance and love alive with your partner. Children, work, housework, and other mundane chores can seem endless, and you both feel exhausted at the end of the day. Just take a minute to remember what dating was like. Counting down the minutes until you saw each other and then that uplifting feeling when you catch sight of your partner.

Recapturing that feeling is the perfect way to raise your inner vibration. Love makes souls soar, and people feel invincible when they are loved.

Take time once a month to have a date night. It sounds corny, but what's wrong with a bit of cheesiness? Choose to dress up, leave the house, and spend a few good hours talking over a chilled-out meal or just a drink.

11) **Become Involved with Your Community:** How well do you know your community? Remember when everybody seemed to know everyone else, and you felt connected to your neighbors? Well, they are still there, and it can be deeply satisfying to feel part of something wholesome.

Here are some key ways you can reconnect with your community:

• *Shop Locally:* Even though it is more convenient to do all your shopping in one big outlet, you lose that sense of connection. Try sourcing your shopping with local stores and visit farmers' markets in your area. The food will be fresher, and you could find real bargains close by.

• *Support Your Local Teams:* Are there any little league teams in your area? Do you have a school or college team playing nearby? You can gain a lot from attending these amateur events. Teams play with spirit and energy, and they will help you feel part of the experience.

• *Visit Local Events:* Is there an outdoor movie screen near you? Check out local papers and Facebook groups to get an idea of events you can attend. You could combine attending a local music festival with date night and turn an ordinary weeknight into an event to remember.

Arts festivals are a great way to connect with your contemporaries. The food will be from mom-and-pop stores, while local artists will be displaying their wares. Stalls will include jewelry, clothing, and other artisan items, and you can get really awesome stuff straight from the creative forces that made them.

Getting involved with your community is an uplifting way to benefit your mind, body, and soul.

Raising your vibration is not meant to be arduous. It should be fun, filled with energy, and a part of making your life more meaningful. When you do not see it as a task but as a joyful exercise, you are already one step on the path to spiritual enlightenment.

Chapter 7: How to Connect with Your Spirit Guides

Spirit guides are the ultimate source of love and light. They are the driving force behind the divine support group that watches over everyone. They know how to push you in the right direction and lead you away from danger. They oversee your every move and are your official cheerleaders in spirit form.

If you have ever felt a calm, soothing presence surround you in times of trouble, this would be your spirit guide, letting you know you are not alone. They have been a part of your life since your conception and will be there even beyond your death. For some people, that is enough. They do not need to make the connection more personal as they are happy to let the guides do their stuff in the background.

Some people are more in tune with their spirit guides. They welcome them into their lives and actively seek a connection. They want you to connect with them and will be open to your efforts, but take warning; it can take time. The key to a successful connection is to chill. Do not get stressed if they don't come through the first time you try to form a relationship.

They know you are trying, but they also know that you may not be ready for such a deeply intense experience. They recognize that you are putting in the effort, but they need to know you are committed to a lasting bond. Think of it as building bridges.

If this all sounds a little farfetched, be reassured that it is possible. You need to make time for your spirit guides if you want a constant source of joy, wisdom, and love in your life.

Step 1: Imagine What You Are About to Experience

Do you remember when you were young and spent hours imagining what the future would hold? What job would you do or what your wedding day would look like? Maybe you dreamt of being an astronaut and floating through space, or your dreams were more practical. Perhaps you imagined being a firefighter or a doctor. Remember the details your imagination conjured up? Well, now is the time to put that imagination to good use.

Too often, people are stuck in their logical adult mindset that does not acknowledge the existence of spirit guides. They need to change that and become more childlike. As a child, there were no boundaries to where one's mind could travel. Everything and anything was possible, and you traveled freely within your thoughts.

Opening your psychic abilities can be tricky when you are in that mindset, so try this exercise to expand your imagination.

Take a Pen and Paper and Write Down These Questions:

- Who are my spirit guides, and when did they live on Earth?
- What are they called?
- Are they young or old?
- What type of personality do they have? Are they fun or serious?

- How many of them are there?
- Do they wear heavenly robes, or do they dress normally?
- Why have they chosen to protect me?
- How old are they?

If you want to make the exercise more intense, choose a sparkly journal and colored pens to jazz up your list. Having a spiritual journal is a great way to record your experiences and reflect on them later.

The main thing to remember is to let your imagination run wild. Draw images of your spirit guides, and then, when you do make contact, you can compare the images with the actual form of your spirit guide. You may be surprised how accurate your drawings are!

Step 2: Set Out Your Intentions

This could be another section of your journal, or you can just do it mentally. Your intentions are a wish list of things you hope to achieve with the help of your guides. Intentions are the starting point of every single dream you have. You cannot complete an action without having an intention.

Basic Intentions That You Can Put on Your List:

- I intend to be more successful at work. I want to learn more skills and become a better leader. My job is important to me, but I also intend to learn how to relax when I get home. Can the spirit guides help me find a natural balance between my work and my need for relaxation?

- I intend to have an energetic body that I treat with respect. I avoid harmful foods, and I exercise regularly. I intend to ask my guides for help in keeping myself fit and free from toxins.

- I intend to have a happy marriage and family life. I will commit to my family with my heart and soul, and I ask that they do the same. Will the spirit guides help me keep my relationships healthy?

- I intend to become a spiritually enlightened being, and I ask the guides for their assistance. Am I on the right path, or do I need to change directions?

- I intend to become a more functioning member of my community. Will it help me become more available to those who need me, or will I be overwhelmed by others' needs? I am asking the spirits for their advice and counsel.

Of course, everybody will have different intentions, and they can be as diverse as you like. The main rules to stick by are to make them pure and attainable. The spirit guides are pretty flexible, but they would not appreciate greedy or self-centered intentions.

Step 3: Ask for Guidance from the Highest Order of Spirit Guides

Like the natural world, there are many different personalities in the spiritual world, and if you are not specific about your intentions, you could get the wrong guide. There are five main types of spirit guides, and they will help you in different ways. Ask for a guide that is tailored to your personal needs at the time of asking.

Main Types of Guides That Can Come to Your Aid:

1) *Guardian Spirit Guides*: These are the spirits you need to keep you physically safe. If you feel your life is in danger from a physical force, call on them to protect you. Guardian guides are always with you and create an energetic shield around you to protect you from danger without being instructed. However, in times of danger, you may feel the need to reinforce their help and feel safer in a dangerous world.

2) *Messenger Guides:* When you reach a crossroads and need advice, you can call on this type of guide to give you the information you need to make an informed decision. They will provide you with insight into the outcomes you can expect by taking a certain path. They will also support whatever decision you make and give you the courage to try new experiences.

3) *Gatekeeper Guides:* These types of guides are there to protect you as you cross into the spiritual world. They will instruct you on methods of spiritual growth and how to tap into your psychic abilities. Gateway guides will help you travel the astral planes without encountering harm and will be there for you when you eventually cross over.

4) *Healing Guides:* While it may seem obvious what these guides do, it needs to be clarified what help they provide. In times of sickness, during surgery, and when the body is in pain, these guides will bring their healing powers. They can use their energy to help the body heal and reduce the strain you feel during illness. However, they are also there for times of emotional stress and will offer spiritual support when you are feeling down.

5) *Teacher Guides:* During your lifetime, you are always learning. You find out exciting new things daily, so imagine how fulfilling having a teaching guide will be. They have a wealth of knowledge and wisdom that help you overcome some of life's biggest challenges. They arm you with a depth of understanding, so you feel ready for whatever life throws at you! They can also help with more practical learning methods and help you develop the concentration to absorb knowledge.

It is important to understand that there are many types of guides for you to call on. Just like the physical world, some spirits are just starting, and some are experienced guides. When you call for an experienced guide, you will probably encounter a few apprentice guides. Just like us, they must learn by experience!

Malignant spirits also inhabit the spiritual world but do not worry about them too much. Safety is covered later in this book, but in general, you call the shots. They cannot invade your spiritual space unless you invite them.

Step 4: Use Prayer and Meditation to Listen More Intently

Thus far, you have learned about vibrations and how they affect your relationship with the spirits. When you have a strong vibration, you can connect with higher beings, but you can be distracted by your vibration's strength and fail to hear what the spirits are telling you. When you slow the vibration, you open your senses to align with the messages you are being sent.

Begin to Set the Tone with a Prayer

"I appeal to my spirit guides to join me in prayer. I ask that they hear my call for help and wisdom and respond to my pleas for aid. I thank the higher beings that embrace my soul and free my self-will. Thank you from my heart."

The Spirit Guide Meditation

While most forms of meditation will slow your vibration and allow the spirits to touch base, this meditation is tailored to connecting with spirit guides. It is a beautiful practice that will fill your soul with love and light as you appeal to the guides to enter your life.

Make sure you have your spirit journal on hand so that you can record in detail any messages you receive.

Now sit up straight in a chair or on the floor with the soles of your feet flat to the ground. Ensure you have no distractions, and no one will enter your space for the next twenty minutes.

Control your breathing until it is the only thing you are aware of. Take deep breaths and then exhale mindfully. Take ten breaths until you feel your heart rate begin to drop.

Let go of your worries. Imagine them as physical objects weighing you down that are tied to your body. Now cut the ties and feel your body become lighter. Imagine them floating off or rolling away from you as you feel them leave your consciousness.

Sink into your inner mind and block out unnecessary chatter that may exist in your head. You may feel slightly nervous at this stage as you think about what might happen. Let it go, remain calm, and breathe slowly to regroup your thoughts.

Welcome the spirit guides into your consciousness with a spoken incantation. "*I welcome those guides of the truth and highest vision that join me today and every day. I thank you for your compassion and wisdom as you guide me through life. I ask you to give me instructions for living a better life and becoming a spiritual being.*" This could be a good time to refer to your intentions if you feel you have a connection.

Invoke the power of choice. While you are still in a meditative state, you can choose to change your mindset to allow spiritual contact. Acknowledge that you have spent your life listening to your mind, and it has made you feel unsatisfied. Now state your intention to open your mind to outside influences.

"*I choose to change the way I listen. I am attuning myself with my spiritual guides and shifting my attention from the earthly world. I recognize that I am a presence with many gifts available to me. Spirits show me the way to discover these gifts and help me grow.*"

Step 5: Believe in Yourself

Recognize your worth. People are constantly being held back by people telling them they are not good enough or don't deserve certain things. When you cast off these beliefs, it gives you the freedom to do great things. The spirit guides believe in you. They know you are capable of greatness and want you to succeed. Sometimes the biggest obstacle in your way is your self-doubt.

Since the moment you took your first breath, you have been part of a team. The gods and goddesses that rule the spiritual realm—and ancestors—make up this team. The angels and archangels that surround you and the spirit guides that look over you are all there for you too. There are multiple souls and spirits invested in you, so why wouldn't you believe in yourself?

Step 6: Write the Spirits

Connecting with spirit guides does not have to be a serious experience. They love fun just as much as you do. Try these fun ways to connect with them, and you may be amazed at the results!

First, you need to get rid of your logical brain. Remember how you entered the imagination zone to picture what your spirit guide looked like? This is a practical extension of the process.

Now take some blank paper, pens, and crayons and just ask them to join you. If you have an idea about whom you want to channel, you can ask them directly using their name or title. For instance, if you know the spirit you want to channel is feminine, you can ask them to join you by saying, "Hey sister, would you care to join me in a creative exercise?"

You may have already prepared some writing prompts to help you. These can be as vague or as detailed as you like. You may prefer to let the words flow unfettered by prompts. The choice is yours.

When you begin to write or draw, you should feel energy guiding your pen. Your handwriting may change, and the tone of the writing may be different. Sometimes the spirits will take the chance to draw you a self-portrait! Do not worry if you aren't arty in the natural world, as you can just let the spirits take over.

Make sure you have a range of materials to create the pictures they want to show you. Experiment with different paints, glitter, and other crafty stuff. The spirits love to spend time flexing their creative muscles! Once they have created these pieces of art or literature, you can hang the results in your sacred space. This will help you have a visual image to focus on during periods of meditation.

Chapter 8: What Happens When the Human Soul Enters the Spiritual World?

First, you must consider how the spiritual world and the natural world coexist. The natural world is where you spend your human life. It consists of everything you see around you—grass, sky, the birds and bees, and your home. The environment is changing with the seasons, and you can feel the sunshine on your face. In the natural world, you are subject to physical and mental harm both from others and yourself.

You experience emotional shifts and moments of deep joy accompanied by moments of sadness. You celebrate the birth of new beings, and you grieve when your loved ones die. But what happens when you die? Is it the end of your being, or is there another stage to your existence?

Sometimes the hardest part of losing a loved one is the feeling you will never see them again. However, what if you could change that? What if you could say goodbye to someone and know it is just a temporary parting?

The spiritual world is filled with people who have passed over. They have bodies and homes and are surrounded by landscapes that resemble Earth. They have communities where they form relationships with kindred spirits, and they can also communicate with the natural world when required.

The difference is that the spiritual world is more vibrant. It is a much more positive environment where thoughts become a reality, and time is irrelevant. There is no stress, just love and peace. The way you live on Earth determines the place you reside in the spiritual world.

What are these facts based on? The spirits. They describe a utopian existence that is waiting for everyone following the transition from the living world. Spiritualists who have connected with their loved ones during readings or meditation describe a place filled with sunlight and warm air that positively glows with love.

So, if death is not the final stage of life, it makes it easier to say goodbye to loved ones when they die. Understanding what the process of transitioning involves can also help you prepare for your death. The biggest fear in life is the unknown. If you have the information directly from the spirits themselves, you know what to expect.

If you plan to contact your departed loved ones during your spiritual awakening, you can ask them about this process and their experiences.

Step 1: Their Ancestors Join Them

Nobody dies alone. The angels and members of their families from the spiritual world join them. When someone is in the process of dying, they have the opportunity to ask for assistance from people on the other side. It is common for a spouse to be there for their partner, along with their parents.

When someone is dying, it is common for them to stretch out their arms as if to embrace people. This is because they can see the people they love welcoming them to the spiritual realm. Dying people will often say the names of their loved ones as they take their final breaths.

Step 2: Spirits Can Leave the Body When the Time is Right

When someone dies during a traumatic experience, the spirit can leave the body even before the physical body is gone. This is because the spirit world is aware that the soul needs respite before the physical body is released during times of suffering. When the loved ones are present during the time of suffering, the spirit can leave the body and join the people who are witnessing the event.

Step 3: The Resting Space

The process of dying can be traumatic and exhausting. Spirits need to rest and recuperate before they go forward into the spiritual realm. Some souls will be suffering from spiritual wounds and need help from designated healing spirits to become whole again. Some people have described this space as the holding spot where spirits are stuck between death and the spirit zone.

This is not strictly true. Spirits need to be whole before they are ready to join their fellow dwellers in the spiritual realm, and this is the place they prepare themselves. They are not stuck or troubled; they are merely resting.

Step 4: The Life Review

This is another misunderstood part of the process. Some people describe this stage as the period of judgment that decides where the soul will go. This makes the process sound much more censorious than it is.

The life review is when the spirit takes time to reflect on their time on Earth. This process can take weeks, months, or even years to complete depending on the individual. This is a process that is essential to help the spirit transcend and enter the spiritual realm. They will be joined by angels and spirit guides to assist them with the review, who will help, not judge.

Imagine a small movie theater with ten seats and a large screen. Here, the spirit is encouraged to say what they really think about how they lived their life. Were they able to lead an open and true existence in their earthly body, or did other people influence them?

Now, they are shown the positive impacts they have had on people. From birth right through to the moment of their death, they will be shown multiple perspectives of the same events. First, they will see things through their own eyes and witness others' reactions as they perceived things. Next, they will see the event from the perception of others.

People often impact others' lives without knowing it, and these occasions are reflected in the life review. If the spirit has done a random act of kindness, the angels will show them the people it affected. This is the ripple effect, and everyone has caused them, but they rarely see the effects in the natural world.

They will then be allowed to review events and times when they did not behave as kindly as they could. It is important to reiterate that this is not a time of judgment; it's a time for reflection. Sometimes you fail to understand how much a throwaway phrase or action can cause hurt to others.

During the review process, the transcending spirit will already be in contact with the community they will be joining after they finish the review. This community will be chosen for them by higher beings depending on their character. Kindred spirits will be placed in communities to create harmony and a lack of friction. During the review process, the spirit can consult with angels, spirit guides, relatives, and their new communities to get a wider perspective about their lives.

It is important to understand that all human souls enter the spiritual world as equals. They will be placed in the community that suits them, depending on their life choices. Nobody is judged, and all religions are treated equally.

The life review process also explains why spirits often take months or years before contacting their loved ones on Earth. Surely the time they are needed most is directly after their passing. The spirit world understands that humans need to heal before they communicate with their loved ones' spirits. They need to have a measure of control and emotional strength to make sure the meeting is not too emotionally charged.

Once the life review process has been completed, the spirit is better equipped to answer any questions their loved ones can ask. They have a deeper perception of how they lived their lives and the impact they had on others. Their wisdom will help them have honest conversations with their human families and explain their former actions.

Step 5: Transcending into Spirit Form

Following the life review, the spirit is now ready to enter the spirit world and decide their role. They are free to explore the different levels of the realm and decide what role suits them best. Some will choose to become spirit guides and make themselves available to human beings seeking their help. Others will choose to become healing spirits and begin to learn from the health deities and angels who are already masters at their work. Spirits who were involved in medicine and the helping professions will sometimes carry on their roles in the afterlife.

Some spirits will dedicate themselves to becoming guides to the family they left behind. They will start to make their presence known by visiting them in their dreams or appearing in animal form.

Some people report that different levels of the spiritual world are accessible by progressing through stages of enlightenment and learning. What is definite is that there is room for every soul in the spiritual world.

The souls that had a more troubled time on Earth and made decisions that others wouldn't have still have a role to play. They can choose to become guides to those on Earth who are currently facing the same decisions they faced. If they can relate to people who are finding life difficult, they can give appropriate advice. If criminals and less savory individuals can receive guidance from people who have made mistakes, they are more likely to follow their advice.

Step 6: Consider Reincarnation

Everyone seeks to become the best version of themselves. However, this cannot be achieved in just one lifetime. Most people have lived multiple lives and must be ready to live many more. All souls want to reach their full capacity to love, help, and receive the full wonders of the universe. This means that spirits are always preparing to return to Earth in another form.

Facts About Reincarnation

The facts below are gathered from people who have experienced multiple past lives and have told how reincarnation works.

- Reincarnation is both natural and universal. You can't opt out because it is how humankind evolves and progresses. The only souls who complete the process and become permanent members of the spiritual world are transcended masters, angels, and deities.

- The actions and decisions you make in a former life don't impact your future lives. Your religion, geographical location, and gender can change.

- Some people are reincarnated within their former family, depending on the timing. Some family members will be reborn as babies within their immediate family.

- Despite popular belief, most past life regressions are reflective of the lives of ordinary people. They could be as long ago as Roman times or as recent as a decade ago. Not everyone was Julius Caesar or an Egyptian Pharaoh in a former life!

- Everyone is accompanied by a group of souls who have a special affinity for each other. These are known as soul mates. They are individuals who will always be there to assist you and give you a grounded feeling.

- Everyone has lived lives as both genders. If you lived a life as a man and then were reincarnated as a woman, this can account for a degree of gender dysphoria and a feeling of not belonging in the body you occupy.

- Traumatic events in a former life will account for some form of distress in current lives. They can leave an impression on the soul that affects their lives for multiple lifetimes.

- Some people have reported suffering a physical trauma in a past life that has left a physical mark in their present life. Birthmarks, moles, and blemishes present at birth can be attributed to past traumas and can fade as they get older. Many diseases, phobias, and life skills are reported to have accompanied a soul through their various lifetimes.

- There is no fixed period between one incarnation and another. Nobody seems to understand who decides the time frame, and some people believe it could be a personal choice.

- Suicide is not punishable in the spirit world. Those who are much wiser than others recognize that it is a decision that everyone can make if they feel the need. It is not regarded as a lack of respect for life; it is merely a chance to start again. Nobody commits suicide without a great deal of thought, and the spirits realize that it shouldn't impact the afterlife.

It is believed that before every reincarnation, there is an extensive planning session. Higher-level guides will assist the spirit in choosing the path it wants to take in its next life. They will be joined by the soul mates they will connect with, and a plan is formed.

If they choose to be born into a life that needs certain skills, their guides will give them instructions to follow. They will then plan specific symbols or actions that will trigger the knowledge they require to become available and overcome obstacles.

During the birthing process of their next life, the spirit will undergo a veiling process that induces amnesia. This allows them to begin their new life with a clean slate unhampered by their past lives. They still have the cues that have been implanted into their psyche for when they need them.

Children can often have residual knowledge of past lives that will manifest as imaginary companions and friends. This will usually stop before the child reaches the age of five, and they will often have no recollection of the relationship.

Here is a story of reincarnation that supports the idea that children have residual memories of a former life.

Ryan Hammons was a young boy born to Christian parents who lived in Oklahoma. In 2009, he suffered a series of disturbing dreams, which led to him waking up clutching his chest and crying. He told his parents that his heart had exploded in Hollywood.

He insisted he lived in a house on a street with the name "rock" in it, and he was big. He told his mom he preferred it when he was big, as he had the freedom to do what he wanted. He described being married five times and his three sons. He mentioned a good friend called Senator Five.

His stories were becoming more lavish as he described meeting Hollywood legends, including Rita Hayworth. He also told his parents about vacations in far-flung places and that he worked in an industry where people would get new names.

His parents didn't believe in reincarnation but were becoming troubled by their son's experiences. His mom obtained a series of books filled with images of Hollywood in the 1930s, and she showed them to her son. He reacted strongly to a picture of screen star George Raft in a publicity photo from 1932. Ryan shouted, "Mom, I worked with him! His name is George, and we did a movie together. That man with a raincoat in the picture is me! That's big for me!"

The man in the picture was identified as Marty Martin; an actor turned agent who died in 1964 from a heart attack. Ryan's mom listed the details that her son had told her and then contacted a renowned psychiatrist in child psychology to help her understand what had happened. His name was Dr. Tucker, and he managed to contact Marty Martins' daughter.

She confirmed that the details Ryan had supplied were accurate and that some of the information was news to her even though it was true. She stated he had lived on North Roxbury Drive, which did indeed have the word "rock" in it, and he had three sons.

Ryan and his parents arranged to meet up with Marty's daughter and have an informal meeting between all parties. However, once at the meeting, Ryan became standoffish and was not interested in participating or connecting with Marty's daughter or sharing any memories with her. Following the unsuccessful encounter, he told his mother that he thought his daughter's energy was "off" and quickly lost interest in the whole subject. Ryan quickly became a normal little boy whose only memories were from the present.

The psychiatrist's explanation suggested that once Marty's spirit had witnessed that the daughter he left behind had moved on, he allowed the reincarnated child to gain closure and forget his existence ever happened.

If people ask themselves about reincarnation, they must ask how it can be that so many people have such vivid memories of former lives if they never happened. How can people, as a race, explain the way they feel about certain individuals? Everyone at some stage in their life has felt a connection with someone that transcends earthly connections.

In the same vein of questioning, how do they explain Déjà vu? The weird feeling that they have been in a certain place when they know they haven't. Could it not be feasible that they visited it in a former life?

Chapter 9: Signs That the Spirits are Knocking and How to Hear Them Clearly

Everyone is naturally curious about the spirit world and what happens after death. Even if it is a passing thought, most people have considered if communicating with the spirit world is possible. The spirits know this, and they will know when your curiosity is ready to be satisfied.

You may not consciously decide to begin communications, but the spirits know when you are ready. Do not worry if that sounds like they are about to invade your mind and make unwanted contact; they won't! What they will do is show you certain signs that should make you aware of their presence. They don't want to alarm you; they are merely telling you that when the time is right, they are there for you.

Understanding these signs can be tricky. Sometimes the spirits are way too subtle for people's earthly senses, and the signs can remain unnoticed as they go about their daily lives. When you understand what type of signs to look for, chances are you will notice them almost immediately.

These signs are not sinister; they are meant to soothe your soul and open your senses. If you do not feel comfortable receiving messages from the other side, that is okay. Spirits are always by your side and will continue to watch over you even if you don't want to make direct contact. Remember that spirits are benevolent creatures that just want the best for people. They are full of love, compassion, and empathy for the humans they have chosen to watch over.

Signs That the Spirits are Trying to Communicate with You

Draughts of Cold Air Without an Obvious Source

Cold spells and chilly air may feel less than welcoming, but it is not a negative sign. The spirits understand that changing the temperature of your environment will get your attention. If you have ever experienced the sensation described as "someone just walked over my grave," a spirit has probably visited you.

Humans are warm-blooded entities, and spirits are pure energy. When both are near each other, the spirits lower the temperature by drawing energy from the air. This type of contact can also cause goosebumps. If you have ever experienced your hair standing on edge or goosebumps as you think of somebody who has died, it could be one of them dropping in to say hello.

How to Say Hello

If the temperature has dropped, and you are rubbing your arms to get warm, say out loud, "Hey there, I know you're here, and that comforts me. I can always wear a sweater to get warm if you want to visit again."

Light Flickering or Bulbs Popping

Often flickering lights and blowing out lightbulbs in the movies are the signs that malignant energy is around. In the natural world, this simply is not true. The flickering of lights can be a sign that your loved ones are trying to tell you they are in the room. The energy they bring will affect all electrical appliances, but the bulbs will sometimes overload and pop!

How to Say Hello

If a familiar face comes naturally to you, do not dismiss it. Say hello back and replace the bulb. Tell the spirits that you don't mind replacing lightbulbs, but can they keep away from your expensive 50-inch flat-screen television! The spirits enjoy humor just as much as people do!

Shadows in the Corner of Your Eyes

Spirits can move in front of you, but if you are not attuned to their energy, they will appear as a subtle shadow. This isn't a direct sighting; it is merely a flicker of shadow that will appear and then disappear in seconds.

How to Say Hello

There is not too much you can do to recreate the moment, so a simple nod to the spirit world will suffice. A salute or a head bob will be enough to tell the spirits you know they are there.

Orbs in Pictures

With the higher quality of cameras and the availability of cameras on smartphones, more and more people are capturing orbs in their pictures. Because they have a camera available more readily, they can capture images that may have missed in the past. Orbs appear as balls of light and can be randomly placed in a room or attached to individuals.

What are these orbs, and what do they represent? They are spirits who have joined you and are letting you know they are present. Cameras capture their energy whenever you cannot see them with the naked eye. They will often be captured at important family gatherings as the spirits help celebrate earthly occasions.

Family weddings, baptisms, christenings, funerals, and birthdays will often involve plenty of pictures being taken. The spirits will appear as orbs just to let you know they are still part of the family and feel the joys and sorrows that you do.

How to Say Hello

Make sure you display your pictures that contain orbs. Most people do not take the time to create physical pictures anymore, and they can sit on the phone for months. Take the time to get prints and put them in frames. Then the spirits know you have got their message, and you welcome their contact.

Phone Ringing Once

Many people struggle to cope with losing a loved one and feel comfort from keeping their number on the contacts list on their phone. Spirits who want to make sure the recipient knows who is trying to contact them will use technology. They can direct their energy to make a smartphone ring just once and then display their number. If this happens, it is not meant to freak you out; it's meant as a sign that they miss you and are ready to communicate if you are.

This type of communication is designed to tell you, specifically, who is trying to get in touch. The spirit might choose this method if you previously spent a lot of time chatting with them on the phone. Maybe they didn't live near you when they were alive and miss your voice on the other end of the line.

How to Say Hello

Hold your phone and say "Hi" when you see their name displayed. Have a conversation with them as if they were on the line. When you react positively to the sight of their name on your device, you are telling them you welcome their contact and have no fear.

Vivid Daydreams

Spirits love to make contact through your subconscious, and this often involves your dreams. If they feel the time is right, they will play with your conscious mind to create vivid images designed to get your attention. They want their message to resonate with you for a reason. Maybe they are trying to warn you that you need to be more vigilant or that someone you love needs you right now. These types of messages are time relevant and should not be ignored.

How to Say Hello

Have a mental conversation with the source of information. If you have questions about the message they are trying to deliver, ask them by voicing them in your head. They can then expand on the information using imagery.

Random Thoughts Appear in Your Head

Have you ever had a thought pop into your head with no explanation at all? Did this thought then become useful later? It could be that the spirits sent you a message knowing you would need the information to help you solve a problem. These thoughts can also be vocalized. So, hearing voices in your head may sound a bit off-kilter, but it could be comforting. If you can hear a voice telling you something, listen carefully because it could be a spirit telling you a message.

How to Say Hello

Have a conversation with them. Simple, right? If they choose to vocalize the message they want you to receive, they will be receptive to verbal messages either in your head or out loud. Make sure you acknowledge them loud and clear.

Moving Objects Around

If you have ever entered a room and felt like somebody had been in and moved stuff, it could be a spirit trying to communicate. If you have changed the furniture around after a loved one has died, they could come back and put it right! Certain objects will be associated with different people, and the spirits can use that fact to remind you they are still with you. Opening drawers and moving ornaments are classic signs that the spirit world is trying to contact you.

How to Say Hello

Speak out in a jovial way. Try saying something like, "Hey you, I know you love that chair and want to see it back in its old place. I will leave it there for today, but it's going back to where I like it tomorrow. If you need to move it again, I understand. I miss you, and I love that you are visiting me. Thank you for coming to visit."

Feathers

Finding feathers is a classic sign the spirit community is trying to reach you. They are common ways that relatives, spirit guides, and angels use to send a message. The spirits use different colored feathers to convey more detailed messages and use colors to give their message deeper insight.

Colored Feathers and What They Mean

- *White Feathers*: These are the simplest form of contact. They can appear in places where birds are present or in a completely bird-free zone. They simply mean that the spirits are there, and they are signaling everything is okay.

- *Black Feathers*: While they may seem like a portentous sign, black feathers are not always negative. They will usually appear when you are having a crisis, and times look bleak. Your spirit guides are telling you they know times are difficult, and they are doing everything they can to help.

- *Yellow Feathers*: This is a positive color to receive. The angels and your spirit guides are telling you that things are going great. They are sending you a message that congratulates you on doing a great job!

- *Pink Feathers*: The angels are showing their humorous side and invite you to rejoice with them. They are reminding you that when you laugh, you are never alone. The spirits enjoy the sense of fun you bring to their energy and your joie de vivre.

- *Blue Feathers*: Blue is the color of serenity and peace. The angels are telling you it's time to take a break and reclaim the calm your life needs. Take their advice and go for a long walk in nature or meditate. Sometimes you need a nudge to step back from your busy schedule and take stock.

- *Red Feathers*: Red is the color of passion and love. The spirits are showing you the path to true love and giving you a hand to find it. They want everyone to find perfect partners and settle down. After all, love is the most powerful way to connect with other humans, and the angels' guidance is better than any dating apps!

- *Green Feathers*: Green is the color of health. Think of nature and the significance of the color, and you will begin to understand what the spirits are telling you. They think you should be paying more attention to your health and looking after number one. After all, most people neglect their health at some point. Maybe you are too busy looking after someone else. A green feather means you should slow down, take stock, and maybe have a checkup.

- *Grey Feathers*: Your team of spirits is constantly working on your behalf. They know the issues in your life that are causing you problems, and they are working to solve them. If they feel you may be losing patience with them, they will send you a gray feather. This means you should be patient and wait for guidance from them.

- *Orange Feathers*: This color feather is a sign that you should work on your sex life! They are also a symbol of creativity, positivity, and the importance of physical connections with your partner. If you receive an orange feather, it could be your spirit guides telling you to reconnect with your partner in the bedroom.

- *Purple*: The angels and spirits understand the importance of recognizing when to acknowledge spiritual growth. If they feel you are recognizing your personal truth and becoming attuned to your personal spiritual growth, they will reward you with the gift of a purple feather.

- *Brown*: This feather is a message that you are becoming more grounded. Brown is the color of the earth and is a peaceful reminder to connect with your roots.

Feather Color Combinations

- *Black and White*: The contrasting colors indicate an inner conflict. The spirits are recognizing your struggles and are sending you a clear message to stay strong. Conflicts will settle, and your life will become calmer soon.

- *Black and Purple*: Your spirituality is off the scale! The inner strength and spirituality you are experiencing are immense. Well done you!

- *Black, White, and Blue*: Change is coming, and the spirits are there to help you. Everyone experiences transitional phases in their lives, and when you do, the guides are there for you.

- *Brown and Black*: The angels and spirits are indicating you have achieved a balance in life that is perfect. You have one foot in the physical world and the other in the realm of the spirits.

- *Brown and White*: This combination is a happy one. You are fully protected from harm, and your wellbeing is assured.

- *Red and Green*: While this combination is usually a wardrobe disaster, in the feathered world, it is quite the opposite. If you receive these colored feathers, you are blessed with good luck. Financial and spiritual prosperity is on its way!

- *Grey and White:* These feathers signify uncertainty. The angels and spirits feel you need to make decisions about your future. Ask them for guidance and signs to make the changes you need.

How to Say Hello

Keep the feathers you are given and use them to decorate your home. Feathers are naturally beautiful and make great decorations. You are telling the spirits that you appreciate their gifts of nature, and you are proud to share them with others.

You Hear Songs That Remind You of a Loved One

Most people acknowledge the importance of music in their life. It can be one of the most powerful triggers to invoke memories of people, times, and places from the past. Most couples have a song that reminds them of their relationship, and the spirits are no different. They know that hearing a certain song will mean you are filled with memories of them, so they will make sure you can hear it when they are near.

How to Say Hello

When you get home, make sure you play the songs you have heard. Say aloud how much you enjoy them and reminisce about the events they remind you of. Music can fill the soul with joy, and it should be played whenever possible.

You Smell Aromas That Take You Back in Time

What do you remember about your grandma's house? The smell of a freshly baked apple pie combined with pipe smoke could be the way your grandparents appear to you in spirit form. Aftershave and perfume smells can transport you instantly back to the first time you met your true love. Smells are particularly evocative when you remember someone who has died. The spirits will use them to remind you of happier times and the fact they are still with you.

How to Say Hello

Acknowledge what you smell and the specific memories that you have. If it is your grandparents, say their names. Welcome them into your heart and tell them how much you miss them.

You Hear Your Name in Random Places

Have you ever been in a crowded place and heard your name being called? Maybe you were in a remote spot with no one else around yet heard someone call you. This is a sure sign that the spirits are nearby. They use natural phenomena to replicate your name, and so you will hear it floating on the wind. They can turn the sound of a babbling brook or the call of a bird into your name.

How to Say Hello

Always react to the sound of your name. Turn around and smile before you carry on with your journey. Raise a hand and say, "Hello." It really is as simple as that. The spirits have singled you out for a personal message, and you should thank them. Say something like, "Hey, I hear you, and I love your energy. Thank you for connecting with me. I appreciate it."

You See the Same Animal All the Time

Do you find that no matter what the weather is or the time of year, you see butterflies wherever you go? If you go to work every morning and see cats wherever you look, it could be a message from the spirits. They love to work with the animal world and reach out to you via the natural world. If you feel an affinity for certain animals, it could be a spiritual connection.

How to Say Hello

Show your love for the spirits by keeping images of your favorite animal close by. If you love elephants, choose a coffee mug with an image of them on it. You can buy bedding, curtains, decorations, and all sorts of knickknacks with animal imagery on them. Filling your home with these images will help you form a stronger connection with the spirit world. You are telling them that you appreciate the effort they have made to connect with you.

Chapter 10: Stay Safe While Communicating

Communicating with spirits can be an uplifting experience, but it also has dangerous aspects. Because you are entering a different energy field, it is important to protect your body and soul from danger. If you fail to take protective measures, different forms of negative energy can damage you. You need to protect yourself from negative entities, psychic attacks, and destructive energy forces.

Almost every negative condition can be traced to another human being. People who radiate negative energy will affect you if you lack protection. You must understand the dangers and how they can impact you. When you enter the spiritual world, you face the same dangers from the physical world. The difference is that the attacks are spiritual rather than physical, but the effects are just as devastating.

Before you consider the physical ways to protect yourself, it's important to consider the basics. You are the center of attraction when you enter the spiritual zone, and you must be in the best emotional shape possible. If you enter the spiritual realm with low vibration, you will attract negative energy. This means you could be subject to attacks from sources of evil that wish you harm.

Finding and strengthening your spirit is the only way to be 100 percent safe. You will find ways to raise your vibrations and strengthen your spirit in another chapter. There, you will learn about the various methods of developing your inner strength and becoming a positive spiritual being.

How to Remove Evil and Negative Energy

Mantras

These are spiritual words or phrases that can be used to clear negative energy from your mind and environment. If you have encountered a particularly negative person who has lowered your vibration, you can use a mantra to clear your energy. Similarly, if your home has been affected by negative energy, you can clear it with a positive chant.

Energy is the driving force of life and is composed of both negative and positive forces. These can be affected by psychic attacks from negative forces, but your inner demons can also affect your levels. Before turning to mantras to boost your life force, it is important to understand why you are experiencing negativity.

Sources That Are Affecting Your Energy

- Past actions that you haven't forgiven yourself for
- Disbelief in the process
- Curses from your enemies
- Negative relationships at home or in the workplace
- Negative emotions you feel about others
- Negative emotions other people feel about you

Mantras can be used to stop these forces from affecting your positive energy by translating your inner thoughts into words. You can use mantras from Hindu or Buddhist texts, but the most effective mantras are from the heart.

For instance, if you feel like your negative feelings for someone else trap you, try creating a mantra to free your mind. "I am trapped by my negative energy regarding my relationship with (insert name), and I am freeing myself from it." Or try saying, "My energy is blocked by the hatred I feel from (insert name), and I now dismiss it from my life."

You are naming your emotions and putting your thoughts into words. The next stage is to create a name for your emotional states. For instance, if you are worried about something, you will become "the worried person," or if you are creatively blocked, you will become "the captive creative one."

Now it is time to change the mindset you are in and release the negative energy. Say out loud, "I release the worried person" and becoming "the assured one," and "the captive creative one" will become "the creatively free person."

To Sum It All Up

When you are creating a personal mantra, you need to follow these stages:

- Recognize your mindset and how it is holding you back.
- Give it a formal name.
- Say you are leaving that mindset behind and entering a new level of energy.
- Thank the energy for allowing you to become more positive.

Of course, there are some daily mantras you can use that are less specific. Try these examples of daily chants to raise your energy levels and fill you with positive emotions.

- I am linked to the universe by my energy. We share the same joys, and I rejoice in this fact.
- I embrace the life force of the Earth and the spiritual realms.
- Today, I will create energy that will benefit the world.
- My life force is strong, and I am filled with joy and love.

White Light Protection

Imagine a physical barrier that is formed around you that repels everything that is thrown at you. Having that kind of protection makes you feel like nothing can touch you. Now imagine how that would feel when you enter the spirit world with that sort of protection. All your fears and concerns will be left behind, and you can feel safe with your spiritual forces.

The white light protection technique allows this to happen. It creates a psychic barrier that will repel negative energy and keep you safe.

Here is how to create your white light protection:

- Sit in a peaceful place and relax.
- Imagine an egg-shaped white sphere filled with light that encompasses your whole being.
- Imagine the negativity hitting the outer layer of light and reflecting away from you.
- Carry this shield with you wherever you go.

This technique is just as effective for your pets, loved ones, and home.

Smudging

Native Americans are thought to have been the first cultural group to use smudging to cleanse their spirits and homes. It is also known as Lakota and Cahuilla. Many other cultures around the globe have used this spiritual ritual for generations.

What Are the Benefits of Smudging?

Antibacterial Properties

While people use the ritual to clean their auras and purify the area they meditate in, there are also practical benefits to smudging. When you use sage or white sage to purify the air, they release antimicrobial properties. These can keep harmful bacteria at bay and repel insects. The antibacterial properties help you maintain a serene area free from infection.

Sage also releases negative ions, which helps you clear common allergens like pet dander, dust, and mold. If you have a respiratory condition, you will find the air cleaner and less likely to aggravate your condition.

It Helps the Quality of Your Sleep

The compounds in traditional sage plants help soothe anxiety and depression. It also calms you and improves your sleep.

It Smells Great

If you prefer natural incense to help you relax, you should burn sage. The aroma is pure, simple and will help your room smell fantastic.

The most important aspect of smudging is to purify your space. This helps you repel negative energy and make sure the positive forces can reach you. There are different herbs for corresponding purposes, and here is a list of useful herbs used for smudging:

- *Angelica:* Promotes self-discovery and strengthens self-resolve

- *Elder:* Protects the area and promotes self-awareness

- *Lavender:* Cleanses, protects, and brings a calm atmosphere

- *Mugwort:* Protects and helps the practitioner remember their dreams

- *St. John's Wort:* Increases courage, protection, and confidence

- *Thyme:* Protects and strengthens the immune system

How to Smudge

Basic Tools

- A bundle of your chosen herb/herbs
- A pot made of natural materials to hold the burning bundle and capture the ashes
- Matches
- A fan made of natural materials to waft the smoke

Now prepare your room for smudging. Remove animals and people who are not participating in the ritual and then open the windows. This allows the smoke to capture the negative energy and then escape.

Light the bundle until it is smoking. Extinguish any flames immediately.

Direct the smoke around your body and head until you feel cleansed.

Now you can use a feather or your fan to direct the smoke to any areas of your body you think need attention.

Collect any ash in your natural pot.

Now cleanse your room by smudging the objects in it. This can be done by directing the smoke over each object individually, or you can leave the smoking bundle in a fireproof container and let the smoke take its natural path.

Once the ritual is completed, extinguish your bundle by placing the lit end in some sand or the ash you have collected. Once it is out, put the remaining bundle away for use in the future.

Safety Tips

Sage can burn quite fiercely, so have some water handy just in case. Never leave it unattended, and be aware that it can set off fire alarms.

Small amounts of smoke are okay but try not to inhale too much, or you could experience adverse reactions. Treat the ritual respectfully, and you will feel the benefits for days after.

Sea Salt as Protection

The natural source of sea salt is, of course, the ocean. These mighty bodies of water have long been regarded as some of the most beautiful natural phenomena on Earth. They are major sources of energy, and the salt they produce has been used for cleansing since the beginning of time. Nearly every culture across the globe uses salt to perform cleansing rituals. From the Catholic Church to ancient Indian religions, salt is part of their holy rituals and ceremonies. The Indians and other cultures applied salt directly to open wounds to remove bad spirits and negative energy.

Salt is a powerful tool and must be used carefully. It has the power to remove psychic energies, but it cannot distinguish between "good" and "bad" energy. This is why it is used to clear a room of energy before rituals and ceremonies to allow the practitioner a clean slate to work with.

Traditionally it has also been used to protect "innocents" from unwanted psychic attacks. Barriers of salt were often placed around children's beds to protect them as they slept. Saltwater is also used to wash magical objects before they are used.

If you want to protect your area before a ritual, you can perform a swift process to give you some level of safety. Light a small fire in a suitable container and throw a handful of sea salt into the flames. You will witness a flash of color, and your immediate area will feel lighter and more spiritual.

If you require a deeper cleanse and have the time to perform the rite, the following magical ritual will give you a deeper spiritual cleanse:

1) Select a bowl or pot made from natural materials, which is a thing of beauty. Size is not as important as energy absorption is not related to volume!

2) Fill the container with salt. Cooking salt will work, but sea salt is better.

3) Place it in the hearth of the home. This can be the kitchen, the room in which you perform rituals, or your bedroom. You know where the heart and hearth of your home is.

4) Leave the salt untouched for three days and nights.

5) On the morning of the fourth day, take your bowl of salt and release it into nature. This can be as majestic as a free-flowing river or as mundane as a garden hoe. It doesn't matter where it goes as long as it goes! As you disperse your salt, tell it your worries. What are your deep-seated negative issues and problems? As the salt disappears, so will your issues.

6) Replace the salt and place it in the hearth.

7) Empty the receptacle every week, and your home will feel the psychic benefits.

Crystals and Gemstones for Protection

When you are choosing crystals to help you protect yourself from negativity and bad spirits, it is important to know which ones are the most effective. As a rule, darker crystals work best for personal safety because they are the most effective at absorbing troubling energy and keeping it away from your positive core.

You can place crystals around your sacred space to ward off evil, or you can wear them as jewelry. There are rods available from online sources that enable you to combine your crystals for handheld protection.

The Best Crystals to Use for Protection and Their Properties

1) **Black Tourmaline:** This is an all-around protection crystal that can repel all lower-level vibrations. This means that spirits and energies that can be malignant will be unable to invade your space. It transmutes negative energy into a positive force. This positivity then surrounds you and acts as a protective parameter to keep bad thoughts and emotions away.

2) **Jet:** Even though it isn't strictly a crystal, Jet is recognized as a powerful tool to protect against darker energies. It is a popular choice for those who have traveled the earthly plane many times since it is renowned for keeping ancient memories. This dark black stone will need regular cleaning as it absorbs more energy than it gives out.

3) **Black Obsidian:** Often used by shamans and witches, this stone is a sharp, effective way to cut ties with the negative forces in your life. You can use it to chip away at lies, bad relationships, and destructive energies. Because it is formed from a volcanic rock when an eruption occurs, it is a powerful combination of all

the Earth's elements. The power that lies in this healing crystal should not be underestimated.

4) **Quartz:** If you prefer a gentler stone to work with, you can choose a smoky version of the popular crystal quartz. Rather than cut through negative energy like the obsidian, it dissolves it until it returns to the earth. Even though it has a gentle essence, it will provide you with powerful protection in the spiritual realm.

5) **Fluorite:** The essence of this crystal is purely protective. It can shield people from electromagnetic stress in the workplace and should be placed near computer screens for a protective barrier. In the spiritual realm, it acts in the same way. Fluorite is effective against any form of negativity. It reflects and absorbs outside forces while cloaking your aura. This protects your activities from harmful sources of energy.

Spiritual Objects

Your sacred place should be the oasis of your life. It is the place you feel the most relaxed and safe. This could mean that you are free from clutter and your area is a clean space, or it could mean the things that make you feel secure surround you. Spirituality is a personal choice, and many beautiful objects look great and provide protection.

If you like to feel comfortable with physical objects representing spirituality, you have a great choice of readily available things.

Ideas for Your Spiritual Makeover

1) **Gargoyle Statues:** If you are a fan of Gothic architecture, you will be familiar with the image of gargoyles. They were regularly placed on buildings to ward away evil spirits and protect the home. Some of them are downright scary, while others are more appealing to the eye! They can be depicted in many ways. Some will be sitting, contemplating, and pondering on life, while others will be fighting dragons with pitchforks.

If you need a fearsome protector for your space, you could choose the traditional image of a poised, protector, winged gargoyle. If you prefer a softer image, try Tristan the sitting gargoyle.

2) **Buddha Statues or Images**: The Abhaya Buddha is traditionally used for protection. The image of Buddha has a different meaning depending on its position. If you want protection, choose a statue in the Abhaya position. This means the Buddha displays the back of his right hand and often holds a lotus flower in his left hand.

The origin of the gesture dates to Buddhist folklore. It is said that Buddha was accompanied by a group of people walking through a forest when an elephant began to charge them. Buddha raised his right hand, so the palm faced his chest, and the elephant stopped its rampage and returned to the forest.

3) **The Sign of the Cross**: Way before Christianity, the cross was used as protection. As far back as the Bronze Age, symbols of the sun cross were used to protect homes.

4) **Hamsa:** Otherwise known as the all-seeing eye, this symbol of a hand with an eye drawn on it is a symbolic representation of the five blessings of spiritual culture. This image can be personalized with additional words and phrases to make the protection level more effective.

5) **Statues of Durga**: This goddess of war is the mother of the Hindu Universe and will protect you from all forms of evil. She has multiple limbs to help her fight negativity from all angles. Representations of Durga differ, and you can choose the one that appeals to your personal vibe. She can be found with bows and arrows, a thunderbolt, a sword, or a lotus blossom, which she uses to vanquish her enemies.

The bottom line is your sacred space, and the journeys you make from there should be safe. The physical world is dangerous, and you make sure you are safe whenever you go out, so why wouldn't you do the same in the spiritual world?

You may feel your spiritual force is a strong, vibrant weapon that can keep negativity at bay. That is fine, but if you are a beginner or have been subjected to negativity, you should arm yourself against further psychic attacks.

The methods above should give you the confidence to enter other realms with confidence. Of course, if you are accompanied by your guardian angels and other spirit guides, you have an extra level of safety.

Chapter 11: Spiritual Places and Times

When you are on a spiritual path, you can feel isolated and alone. You will be breaking free from some parts of your life and choosing a new footpath. Sometimes you will need reminders about why you are on your journey and what you can expect along the way.

When you communicate with the spirits, your mind needs to be at peace, filled with hope and joy, and ready to receive their messages. This book has already discussed different ways to enhance your life, but what else can you do?

Revisiting your inner child is an essential part of letting go of your fear. As children, people believed the world was magical, and they could do anything they wanted. They did not have restrictions, and their imagination was vivid. They played when and where they wanted, and they were eager to learn new things. You have already learned about the importance of imagination and a childlike attitude when seeking a spiritual connection, so now you can explore some ways to become connected with your inner child.

Everyone is constantly reminded that their childhood was possibly the happiest time of their lives, so what can you do to remember those times?

Ways to Recapture the Joys of Your Childhood

Visit your old school and bring back memories of early friendships and the glee you felt when you saw your friends. Childhood friendships were simple and uncomplicated. You liked the people you felt an affinity with, and the camaraderie you had felt like it would last a lifetime.

• **Build a Swing in Your Garden**: There is a certain type of freedom you feel when you sit on a swing. That euphoric sense of reaching for the skies will help you let go of all your woes.

• **Experience Your Emotions**: When people get older, they become more self-conscious. They are afraid to let go of their emotions and show how they really feel. Remember what used to make you laugh when you were a child and revisit it. Maybe you loved a certain cartoon, like Roadrunner or Tom and Jerry. Try watching a couple of episodes and laughing raucously. When you laugh with your body, you experience an overwhelming feeling of joy.

• **Take Time to Relax**: When was the last time you chilled without worrying about what the future holds? Take a weekend break in the countryside with your friends or family and let go of your worries. Swim in the sea, play games, build an open fire, and roast marshmallows while you swap stories by the fireside. You could go the extra step and camp outside to get the most from your experience.

• **Spend Time with Children**: When you talk with young children, you remember what it felt like to be young. Their enthusiasm and optimism bubbles over and fills their speech with such hope. Play games with them and recapture your youth. Hide and seek or climb a tree to help you reset your mind space and fill you with an innocence you may have forgotten existed.

- **Visit Childhood Haunts**: Was there a house in your neighborhood that all the kids thought was haunted? Did you have butterflies in your belly every time you walked past it? Maybe there was a tree you used to climb or some woods you used to camp out in. Revisit them and become the free spirit you were back then.

- **Dance Like a Child**: This is an effective way to recapture your inner child. Put some music on that is loud, fast, and catchy, and then dance. Not just shuffling about looking self-conscious but really letting go. Raise your arms on high and kick those legs out while you sing along with the music.

Spiritual Places to Visit

Travel definitely broadens the mind, but what about your spiritual side? Some amazing destinations on Earth are filled with images that can fill your soul with wonder. You may dream of visiting them but cannot envision a time when this will be possible. Why shouldn't you be able to visit wherever you like? Sometimes people stop imagining and dreaming and concentrate on managing their expectations. What if you believed that anything was possible, and the world was your oyster?

Dare to dream. One day you will have the chance to visit some of these amazing spaces, and you will grasp that chance. In the meantime, surround yourself with images of these places and let your mind imagine yourself there. If you want a more visual aid, use technology to transport you. Google Earth will place you wherever you like in a matter of seconds! If you want to transport yourself to the peak of Everest, you can!

Some of the Most Inspirational Places on Earth

Borobudur, Indonesia

This magnificent Buddhist monument is located on the island of Java. It is designed to represent a three-dimensional map of the universe. The ten levels of construction can take days to explore fully. The area is filled with natural beauty, and travelers to the area have multiple opportunities to enjoy them. You can take a sunrise jeep tour that begins with a view of the sunrise in Borobudur, followed by a tour of the nearby Mount Merapi and a four-wheel drive excursion well into the afternoon.

You can also book a four-day tour of the area for under $400, including a pickup from central Java that continues across the island. You can see the impressive waterfalls at Tumpaksewu and then explore the Mt. Bromo volcano. The tour involves a hike to the Ijen crater, the home of the legendary blue fire caused by the unique acid lake it houses.

Macchu Picchu, Peru

This fifth-century citadel is one of the most remote sites on Earth. It sits atop the Sacred Valley on a mountain ridge nearly 2,500 meters above ground level. Visitors will most likely stay in the city of Cusco, and travel to the citadel is varied. You can take a bus or train to Macchu Picchu or take advantage of hotel pickups. The Festival of the Sun is one of the best times to visit the area as it marks the New Year celebrations the Incas followed. The Festival begins on June 21 and carries on until the 24th. The Sun stays in the same place for three days, and when it rises on June 24, it marks the celebration known as Inti Raymi.

Lourdes, France

At the foot of the Pyrenees lies the small marketing city of Lourdes. It is believed the Virgin Mary appeared to a young girl named Bernadette eighteen times at the Grotto of Massabielle. She appeared as a light-bathed young woman who was clothed in robes of white. The area is, as the locals would say, Magnifique! There are numerous religious activities to take part in, like the Candlelight procession that happens every day or the Basilica that symbolizes the Immaculate Conception.

Lourdes is especially appealing to people who are unwell or have been disabled in some way. The spring discovered near the grotto is said to contain healing properties and is visited by over five million pilgrims every year. Tales of miraculous healing are attributed to the waters that flow there.

Stonehenge, England

Deep in the Wiltshire countryside is possibly one of the most amazing pieces of construction in Europe. This prehistoric site is home to an ancient spiritual site that once formed a perfect circle of stones aligned to mark the solstices. It was attributed to Druids but has since been found to predate their religion by 2,000 years or more.

Despite this fact, present-day Druids gather there to celebrate the midsummer solstice. They are joined by huge numbers of tourists that are eager to see the spiritual landmark. The stones are all over twenty tons in weight and were sourced over eighteen miles away from the site. Experts still don't know exactly how they were transported. Visitors to the site refer to it as a "power place" imbued with spiritual healing powers. Stonehenge is a magical place, and you can feel the presence of the spirits that reside there.

Chichen Itza, Mexico

In the southern part of Mexico lies an archaeological site built by the Mayan people in the early part of 400 AD. The city was believed to have housed over 3,500 people and was dominated by a large cenote at the northern end, a site rumored to have been designated for human sacrifices. When the area was dredged in the early 1900s, it yielded numerous human remains and great treasures. While its inhabitants abandoned the city in the 1200s, the remaining structures helped establish its significance as an architectural site in the 1800s.

The site is a unique record of the Mayan civilization and their culture. It was declared a UNESCO heritage site in 1988 and was more recently declared one of the modern wonders of the world.

Structures You Can Visit at Chichen Itza

- *El Castillo*: This temple is dedicated to a Mayan deity that took the form of a snake with feathers. The temple has a pyramid design that was built from limestone. Its impressive form dominates the site and is truly breathtaking.

- *The North Temple*: This is also referred to as the Temple of the Bearded Man because of the carving within its inner walls. Visitors can view this image of the feathered serpent surrounded by warriors carrying weapons on the back wall, while the central wall shows a man with a carving under his chin that resembles facial hair. Although the temple is small, it is beautifully decorated and shows depictions from Mayan culture.

- *Temple of the Warriors*: Another magnificent step pyramid, this temple depicts different images on every stage. These include warriors in traditional armor ready to defend the temple if required. There are also images of eagles and jaguars devouring human hearts. The temple is meant to be intimidating, and it is!

Chichen Itza covers a huge area that is filled with amazing sights. It may only be 120 miles away from bustling Cancun and the bars and nightclubs, but it is thousands of years away from modern culture.

Mt. Athos, Greece

This spiritual retreat will not appeal to feminists considering it only allows men over the age of eighteen to visit, but when you understand how the monastery operates, the reasoning for their entrance rules becomes apparent. This monastery was established in 1963, so it is relatively modern, but it's considered an important center of the Greek Orthodox Church.

It is set in an area of outstanding natural beauty and houses some of the most treasured artifacts in Greece. They hold spiritual workshops that appeal to all beliefs and provide their visitors with an insight into their spiritual journeys. The monastery is the site of over twenty different communities, and it allows them to exist without governmental interference.

Mecca, Saudi Arabia

Muslims regard Mecca as the holiest city of Islam. The phrase "mecca" has been used in modern language to describe a place that attracts people with similar interests. For instance, "London is a mecca for fashion seekers." Though, the actual holy city is much more than this.

Located in the Sirat Mountains, it is so sacred that only Muslims are allowed into the city. Devout Muslims will attempt to visit the city at least once in their lifetimes and visit the holy mosques located throughout the cityscape. Wherever in the world Muslim people pray, they direct their bodies to face this holy place.

Sedona, Arizona

If you want to witness one of the most dramatic landscapes ever, head to the Arizona desert and visit Sedona. Here you will find the Chapel of the Holy Cross that is spectacularly lit when the Sun sets behind the horizon. The area is filled with energy vortexes and offers the chance to expand your spiritual and mental sense of exploration. Let the natural beauty wash over you as you get some red earth on your hiking boots!

Take a hike over the Boynton Canyon and swim in the Slide Rock State Park as you take in the amazing scenery. You can take a horse ride through the iconic rock formations while you follow in the footpaths of the generations of native Indians who have gone before. There are several holistic courses available to help you feel this amazing place's vibe and help you gain spiritual enrichment.

India

If you seek a spiritual place to inspire you, you should try and visit India. It is filled with religious sites and amazing places of inspiration. Try Mount Arunachala, where pilgrims visit and circle the mountain to clean the psychic karma from all their previous lives. There are eight different temples and caves filled with cosmic vibrations that offer perfect places to meditate.

India also boasts a holy river named the Ganges, and its source has long been thought of as one of the most spiritual places on Earth. Visitors must hike for almost sixteen miles through unforgiving landscapes to reach the source and reach the most revered point in Hindu teachings.

The temple at Bodh Gaya surrounds a tree that is believed to be a direct relative of the tree of enlightenment that allowed Prince Siddharta to ascend to the heavens according to Hindu teachings. Visitors wait for hours to capture one of the leaves that fall from its branches because they believe it offers them spiritual benefits. There are also places to pray and meditate in this tranquil area, surrounded by nature's beauty.

The bottom line must be that everyone would love to have a budget that allowed for travel to these mystical places. They would love to visit the holy city of St. Peters or the Hill of Tara in Ireland. Inspiration lies within all the world's continents, from Iceland's snowy peaks to the magnificent Uluru in Australia. You know they exist, and this means you can draw on their benefits.

The most beneficial spiritual place lies deep within you, and you can take the time and effort to find it. Feed your spiritual hunger with images and details of these special places, and you may find yourself in a position to witness them firsthand. The journey to your more enlightened self-starts with a single step. Nevertheless, the many steps you take after that are your choice.

Conclusion

Imagine how it felt when people discovered the world was not flat. Now consider just how it feels to discover that there is a whole realm within your reach filled with wonder and magic. If you practice using safe methods, there is a place where you can benefit from a host of beings that have lived before you; benevolent spirits who have chosen you to be the one they protect. Spirituality may not be for everyone, but it is available to all.

No matter how you have conducted your life so far, it is never too late to change. Everyone enters the spiritual realm with a clean slate and the old-fashioned belief that the spirits judge has been disproved.

You are about to take an amazing journey, good luck and enjoy the ride!

Here's another book by Mari Silva that you might like

Clairvoyance

The Ultimate Psychic Development Guide to Extrasensory Perception and Intuition

MARI SILVA

Your Free Gift (only available for a limited time)

Thanks for getting this book! If you want to learn more about various spirituality topics, then join Mari Silva's community and get a free guided meditation MP3 for awakening your third eye. This guided meditation mp3 is designed to open and strengthen ones third eye so you can experience a higher state of consciousness. Simply visit the link below the image to get started.

https://spiritualityspot.com/meditation

References

Chopra. "Welcome to the new Chopra." Accessed?. http://www.chopra.com

Hay House. "Daily Affirmations & Inspirational Stories, Meditations, & Videos By Hay House Authors." Accessed?. http://www.healyourlife.com

Forever Conscious. "Forever Conscious." Accessed?. https://foreverconscious.com/

Gabrielle Bernstein. "Gabby Bernstein - #1 NYT Best Selling Author, Speaker & Spirit Junkie." Accessed?. http://gabbybernstein.com

Perfectly at Peace. "Home - Perfectly at Peace." August 6, 2017. https://perfectlyatpeace.com/

LonerWolf. "Walk the path less traveled * LongerWolf." Accessed?. https://lonerwolf.com

LostWaldo. "LostWaldo." Accessed?. https://lostwaldo.com/

ScoopWhoop. "ScoopWhoop - Breaking News, Trending News & Latest Bollywood News." Accessed?. http://www.scoopwhoop.com

United Church of God. "United Church of God." Accessed?. https://www.ucg.org/